I0132509

Classic Rock Woodstock And The Bands That Saved Us From The Beatles

Lessons from Z's School of Hard Rocks

Tom Zalaski

Nantucket Sleighride Productions

Copyright 2016 by Tom Zalaski

Published in the United States by Nantucket Sleighride Productions.

Worldwide distribution facilitated for Nantucket Sleighride Productions by Amazon.com, Amazon Kindle and TomZalaski.com.

All rights reserved. No part of this book may be reproduced by any mechanical, photographic or electronic process, or in the form of a photographic recording; nor may it be stored in a retrieval system, transmitted, or otherwise be copied for public or private use – other than for "fair use" as brief quotations embodied in articles and reviews – without prior written permission of the publisher.

Library of Congress Cataloging-In-Publication Data

Zalaski, Tom
  Classic Rock Woodstock And The Bands That Saved Us From The Beatles / Tom Zalaski. – 1st ed.
ISBN 978-0-9789223-4-4 (paperback)
ISBN 0-9789223-4-4 (Amazon Kindle)

Paperback ISBN 978-0-9789223-4-4
Amazon Kindle 0-9789223-4-4

Printed in the United States of America

**To Leslie West,
Felix Pappalardi
and Corky Laing**

**Thank you for a lifetime
of music and memories**

True hardcore rockers will understand

THE PLAYLIST

Introduction

The Rockin' Chair's Rockin'!

Hell no, we're not old! We're still here, we're still rockin' and we're not goin' away anytime soon! Greetings, fellow aging rockers!

Yes, we've got gray hair (or maybe no hair!), our kids are gone, our grandkids are our whole world, we're retired or at least close to it and too many of our high school friends are getting their pictures in the newspaper on the obituary page to which we say, "Hell no, not me!"

We are classic rock. We are Woodstock. Rock is in our blood. It's a big part of who we are and always have been. It's our identity.

Our kids, grandkids, family members and co-workers don't understand that although we're pushing 65 or 70 years old our rock minds are still 18. When Alice Cooper came out with *I'm Eighteen* we *were* 18!

We still remember the call letters of the first Top-40 rock radio station we listened to. We can recite lyrics to songs we first heard on that station 50 years ago. We still remember our first home phone number and probably the phone numbers of one or two of our childhood friends.

When we watch music awards shows we shout in unison, "What the fuck is that!?" and we ask, "Where are the guitars and why are those people running around the stage lip-synching songs and wearing headsets that make them look like they work at the pick-up window at McDonald's?"

The only person we recognize at the Grammy Awards is the guy who is receiving a Lifetime Achievement Award.

In our world, the word 'rap' begins with a capital C.

At my age music has made me feel cool and old at the same time. As we drove in the SUV one day Van Halen's *Eruption* came on the radio which is followed by *You Really Got Me*. My teenage son and his friends were amazed that I knew the lyrics to *You Really Got Me*. I proceeded to tell them about a 60's band called The Kinks.

Another time when I picked the kids up from school Joe Cocker's *Little Help From My Friends* came on the radio. I blurted out, "Woodstock!" The kids shouted, "Wonder Years!"

And then there was the time a McCartney song came on the radio and one of the kids exclaimed, "Didn't he used to be with Wings?"

I had so much fun writing this book and I hope you have fun reading it. It is a compilation of rock and roll trivia along with more than 100 short stories of the stuff you never knew about the songs, bands and events that shaped us from our teens right up to this day.

This book was actually born on radio. I am a television news anchorman who also does a drive-time radio newscast on 105.7 WAPL-FM in Appleton, Wisconsin. Each Friday I do a feature called 'Z's School of Hard Rocks' where I focus on a musical group, a song or an event like Woodstock. The goal of each vignette was to give my classic rock/Woodstock nation listeners a fun and interesting "I never knew that" story. This book is a compilation of all the stories I did on the radio show.

Along with these stories I have also included news, observations and memories for all of us to share.

I'm so glad you're here. I'm so glad *we're* here! We are the true rock generation. We are hardcore. We know the lyrics to songs most of our peers never heard of. Those songs are our anthems. When Jefferson Airplane's *White Rabbit* comes on the radio we turn up the volume to 11!

I hope you have as much fun reading this book as I did writing it! I'd love to hear from you at www.tomzalaski.com.

"...remember what the dormouse said,
feed your head, feed your head, feed your head."

I don't understand how I can remember every word of a song from 1964, but I can't remember why I walked into the kitchen.

The World's First Corporate Boy Band

I have always contended that the reason the Beatles took America by storm when they first appeared on the Ed Sullivan show on the evening of February 9, 1964 could be traced to one of the most tragic events in U.S. history.

The assassination of President John F. Kennedy in Dallas, Texas on November 22, 1963.

Kennedy's assassination and the three days of public mourning that followed put our country in a state of near national depression. We didn't feel very thankful on that Thanksgiving. Christmas was far from merry. The New Year was less than happy.

The Beatles' appearance on the stage of CBS Studio 50 that Sunday night was the perfect medicine we needed to cure us of the national malaise caused by what happened in Dallas just 77 days earlier.

When Ed Sullivan introduced the band that evening it sent shockwaves through America's living rooms. Parents watched in disbelief and disgust! The long hair! Teenage girls screaming, crying and fainting as if possessed by the devil! Four mop-topped twenty-something musicians singing about wanting to "hold your hand." And what was this "Yeah, yeah, yeah" stuff?

Meanwhile, the sons and daughters of these shell-shocked parents were mesmerized. The music. The excitement. The never-before-heard harmony of "How could I dance with another Ooooooo", the kids begging their parents, "Please, can we stay up a little longer? They're coming back on later!"

The minute the Ed Sullivan show ended at 9 o'clock that night (EST) our national dialogue had changed. The Kennedy assassination had taken a backseat to the Beatles. Dinner table and coffee shop conversations now centered on whether the Beatles had ushered in an exciting new era of music and entertainment or the end of civilization as we knew it!

For those of us who watched the Ed Sullivan Show that night but whose memories have faded and for those who weren't born yet, here are a few facts I hope you'll find interesting.

The Ed Sullivan Show was watched by 73 million television viewers that night. As we watched the screaming and pandemonium in the theater it looked as if there were thousands and thousands of delirious teens in the audience. In fact, there were only 728 people in the crowd. They were the lucky ones because 50,000 ticket requests were received for that particular show.

CBS News anchorman Walter Cronkite used his considerable influence at the network to score two tickets for his daughters who got to meet the Beatles backstage.

The other performers unlucky enough to be booked on the show that night included:

- Dutch comic magician Fred Kaps who performed card tricks and a salt shaker stunt.

- The cast of the Broadway musical "Oliver" who performed several numbers.

- Comedian Frank Gorshin did an impression skit.

- Tessie O'Shea performed three songs including her hit, "Two-Ton Tessie from Tennessee."

- The comic team of Mitzi McCall and Charley Brill.

- Wells and the Four Fays, a comic acrobat team.

The Beatles sang:

- All My Loving

- 'Til There Was You

- She Loves You

- I Saw Her Standing There

- I Want To Hold Your Hand

CBS Studio 50 was later renamed The Ed Sullivan Theater which was home to The Late Show With David Letterman.

How We Learned of John Lennon's Murder

How did the world learn of the murder of John Lennon? Was it announced in a bulletin by CBS News anchorman Walter Cronkite? Was it Harry Reasoner of ABC News? Dan Rather? Peter Jennings? Barbara Walters?

No, the world learned that John Lennon had been killed from a most unlikely source – none other than ABC sportscaster, the inimitable Howard Cosell!

It was the night of December 8, 1980 during the final moments of regulation during the Monday Night Football game between the Miami Dolphins and the New England Patriots.

Here is Cosell's announcement:

"Yes, we have to say it. Remember this is just a football game no matter who wins or loses. An unspeakable tragedy confirmed to us by ABC News in New York City. John Lennon, outside of his apartment building on the west side of New York City, the most famous, perhaps, of all the Beatles, shot twice in the back. Rushed to Roosevelt Hospital. Dead on arrival."

The Beatles Take A Back Seat

I got caught up in the Beatlemania craze just as much as the next 5th grade kid did. After watching the Beatles on Ed Sullivan on that February 9, 1964 evening I couldn't wait to go out and buy the 'Meet The Beatles' album. However, two other items I just *had* to have didn't quite fit into the family budget - the black turtleneck shirt and the Beatle boots.

Yet, less than a year from that day, I had turned my back on the Beatles!

Some new songs were being played on WDRC in Hartford, Connecticut, my local Top-40 radio station. They weren't Beatles songs. These songs were different. I began to realize this new music was more interesting than the Beatles 'moon in June', boy-meets-girl, I love you lyrics.

I didn't know it at the time but this new music would be the foundation of my hard core rock and roll roots that are still part of me today. I know you probably feel the same way, so let's takge a walk down memory lane!

Song	Artist	Year
She's Not There	Zombies	1964 (September)

Just 7 months after the Beatles invaded America, Rod Argent and The Zombies gave us the first indication that there was something out there beside "Yeah, yeah, yeah." It was the first time we heard a band inhale loudly as they belted out the lyrics.

| Have I The Righ | The Honeycombs | 1964 |

While not heavy or psychedelic, the song ushered in a phenomenon we had never seen before – a female drummer, Honey Lantree!

Lies   The Knickerbockers   1965

Remember their vocals? We thought the song was done by the Beatles.

Eve of Destruction   Barry McGuire   1965

Perhaps our first social consciousness song.

Friday On My Mind   The Easybeats   1966

Easybeats guitarist George Young was the older brother of ACDC's Angus and Malcolm Young.

Wild Thing   The Troggs   1966

Too Much To Dream The Electric Prunes   1966

7 and 7   Is Love   1966

Fronted by Arthur Lee, Love delivered a guitar explosion and lyrics that blew the lid off anything we had heard before.

Psychotic Reaction   Count Five   1966
Alice Cooper covered this one.

Talk Talk   Music Machine   1966
Alice Cooper covered this one, too!

Incense and Peppermint   Strawberry Alarm Clock   1967

The name of the song and the artist had 'psychedelic' written all over them!

Kicks   Paul Revere and the Raiders   1967

The first anti-drug song.

Itchycoo Park   Small Faces   1967

You Keep Me Hanging On   Vanilla Fudge   1967

A bit different than The Supremes version!

White Rabbit   Jefferson Airplane   1967

Sunshine of Your Love   Cream   1967

Time (Has Come Today)   Chambers Brothers 1968

Crimson and Clover   Tommy James/Shondells   1968

Pat Benatar covered this.

Spirit In The Sky   Norman Greenbaum   1969

The Legends Are Leaving Us

We children of the 60's and the Woodstock Generation will always remember these three legends as well as where we were and what we were doing when we learned of their deaths.

Jimi Hendrix - November 27, 1942 - September 18, 1970 (age 27) asphyxia (choked to death while intoxicated with barbiturates)

Janis Joplin - January 19, 1943 - October 4, 1970 (age 27) heroine overdose

Jim Morrison - December 8, 1943 - July 3, 1971 (age 27) official cause is heart failure due to accidental overdose of heroine in a ruling that remains disputed

As we approach the 50th anniversary of their deaths I marvel at their unique talent and the enduring music they left us with. They were just 27! Yet, to this day *Purple Haze, Piece of My Heart* and *Light My Fire* stand as anthems of our generation. I feel like a comparative failure when I realize at age 27 my only claim to fame was that I had accumulated some fairly substantial college loan debt!

However, while I am not a music legend, I am glad to be alive which brings us to the story of how Jimi Hendrix and Ted Nugent used to be at cultural and verbal odds. Nugent was put off by Hendrix' drug use and Hendrix used to make fun of Nugent's penchant for camoflage and hunting.

Nugent got the last laugh. Upon Hendrix' death Nugent penned this poem:

Jimi did drugs and now Jimi's dead.

I went huntin', I'm still Ted.

Most of us were in our late teens or early 20's when these three performers left the stage for good. But while we may have been saddened by their deaths, we had no cause to reflect on our own mortality. Afterall, we were young and our own life expectantcy was the last thing on our minds. The passing of Hendrix, Joplin and Morrison, all at age 27, really didn't surprise us. They were the poster children for the drug culture and all three met their demise by living that culture to the extreme. There was a certain degree of logic as to how they met their fates.

But fast forward forty years and we see the deaths of our rock heroes differently, don't we? We and they are in our 60's and 70's and our music idols are not dying of drug overdoses - they're dying of old age!

Richie Havens *can't* be gone! We still see him opening the Woodstock Music and Arts Festival in his flowing robes and his sandals that left marks on the stage from tapping his foot so hard during *Freedom - Motherless Child.*

Alvin Lee of *I'm Goin' Home* fame has gone Home. We still see him on that Woodstock stage with Ten Years After, the young, fair-haired guitar whiz who played the instrument faster than anyone we had ever seen. We could see his breath in the night time air as he sang and played for those nine minutes that would go down in rock and roll history.

Johnny Winter, the legendary albino bluesman is gone. *Rock And Roll Hootchie Coo* will forever be burned in our memories as will Winter's rendition of *Jumpin' Jack Flash* that made the Rolling Stones sound like the Archies.

The unmistakable voice of Jack Bruce of Cream has forever been silenced. *Sunshine of Your Love* and *White Room* are anthems that live on to this day.

And finally, Joe Cocker. We can still see him on that stage at Woodstock playing his air guitar, hands and fingers contorted, arms flailing and face twisted as he asked for *A Little Help From My Friends*.

Havens, Lee, Winter, Bruce and Cocker. We grew up with them. We're as old as they were and their passings remind us of the uncomfortable reality or our own mortality.

Richie Havens - January 21, 1941 - April 22, 2013 (age 72) heart attack

Alvin Lee - December 19, 1944 - March 6, 2013 (age 68) complications from routine heart surgery

Johnny Winter - February 23, 1944 - July 16, 2014 (age 70) emphysema and pneumonia

Jack Bruce - May 14, 1943 - October 25, 2014 (age 71) liver disease

Joe Cocker - May 20, 1944 - December 22, 2014 (age 70) lung cancer

A Woodstock Primer

The song *Woodstock* was written by someone who wasn't even there!

First, some background.

The Woodstock Music and Arts Festival was held August 15, 16 and 17 (due to inclement weather the festival was extended to August 18th) on the 600-acre farm of Max Yasgur in Bethel, New York.

Thirty-two acts performed at the festival. Ticket prices were $18 in advance and $24 at the gate for all three days. Attendance numbers vary between 200,000 and 400,000, most of whom did not pay to get in.

The name Woodstock has always had an earthy, hippie, back-to-nature feel to it. But in fact, the name Woodstock was all about money. The reason the event was called 'Woodstock' was because an investment company known as Woodstock Ventures put up the money to put the show on.

The song *Woodstock* became a huge hit for Crosby, Stills, Nash and Young. But CSN&Y didn't write the song. Graham Nash's then-girlfriend Joni Mitchell did.

Mitchell did not perform at Woodstock because her manager told her it would be more advantageous to her career to appear on *The Dick Cavett Show* instead.

Mitchell's inspiration for the song came from what she heard from Nash about Woodstock and from televised news reports about the festival that she watched from her hotel room in New York City.

The band Matthews Southern Comfort whose leader was Ian Matthews of Fairport Convention fame did a cover of the song.

Woodstock

I came upon a child of God
He was walking along the road
And I asked him, where are you going
And this he told me
I'm going on down to Yasgur's Farm
I'm going to join in a rock 'n' roll band
I'm going to camp out on the land
I'm going to try an' get my soul free
We are stardust
We are golden
And we've got to get ourselves
Back to the garden

Then can I walk beside you
I have come here to lose the smog
And I feel to be a cog in something turning
Well maybe it is just the time of year
Or maybe it's the time of man
I don't know who l am
But you know life is for learning
We are stardust
We are golden
And we've got to get ourselves
Back to the garden

By the time we got to Woodstock
We were half a million strong
And everywhere there was song and celebration
And I dreamed I saw the bombers
Riding shotgun in the sky
And they were turning into butterflies

Above our nation
We are stardust
Billion year old carbon
We are golden
Caught in the devil's bargain
And we've got to get ourselves
Back to the garden
Songwriters: MITCHELL, JONI
Woodstock lyrics © Sony/ATV Music Publishing LLC

The Woodstock Lineup

Day One: Friday, August 15, 1969

Richie Havens

1. Minstrel From Gault
2. High Flyin' Bird
3. I Can't Make It Anymore
4. With A Little Help
5. Strawberry Fields Forever
6. Hey Jude
7. I Had A Woman
8. Handsome Johnny
9. Freedom (Motherless Child)

Sweetwater

1. Motherless Child
2. Look Out
3. For Pete's Sake
4. Day Song
5. What's Wrong
6. Crystal Spider
7. Two Worlds
8. Why Oh Why

Bert Sommer

1. Jennifer
2. The Road To Travel
3. I Wondered Where You'd Be
4. She's Gone
5. Things Are Going My Way
6. And When It's Over

7. Jeanette
8. America (first standing ovation at Woodstock)
9. A Note That Read
10. Smile

Tim Hardin

1. Misty Roses
2. If I Were A Carpenter

Ravi Shankar

1. Raga Puriya-Dhanashri / Gat In Sawarital
2. Tabla Solo In Jhaptal
3. Raga Manj Kmahaj / Alap Jor / Dhun In Kaharwa Tal / Medium & Fast Gat In Teental

Melanie

1. Beautiful People
2. Birthday Of The Sun

Arlo Guthrie

1. Coming Into Los Angeles
2. Walking Down The Line
3. Amazing Grace

Joan Baez

1. Joe Hill
2. Sweet Sir Galahad
3. Drug Store Truck Driving Man
4. Swing Low Sweet Chariot
5. We Shall Overcome

Day Two: Saturday, August 16, 1969

Quill

1. They Live the Life
2. That's How I Eat
3. Driftin'
4. Waitin' For You

Country Joe McDonald

1. I Find Myself Missing You
2. Rockin' All Around The World
3. Flyin' High All Over The World
4. Seen A Rocket
5. Fish Cheer / I-Feel-Like-I'm-Fixing-To-Die-Rag

John B. Sebastian

1. How Have You Been
2. Rainbows All Over Your Blues
3. I Had A Dream
4. Darlin' Be Home Soon
5. Younger Generation

Keef Hartley Band

1. Believe In You
2. Rock Me Baby
3. Leavin' Trunk/Halfbreed/Just To Cry/And Sinnin' For You

Santana

1. Persuasion
2. Savor
3. Soul Sacrifice

4. Fried Neckbones

Incredible String Band

1. Catty Come
2. This Moment Is Different
3. When You Find Out Who You Are

Canned Heat

1. I'm Her Man
2. Going Up the Country
3. A Change Is Gonna Come
4. Leaving This Town
5. The Bear Talks
6. Let's Work Together
7. Too Many Drivers at the Wheel
8. I Know My Baby
9. Woodstock Boogie
10. On the Road Again

Grateful Dead

1. St. Stephen
2. Mama Tried
3. Dark Star / High Time
4. Turn On Your Lovelight

Leslie West & Mountain

1. Blood Of The Sun
2. Stormy Monday
3. Theme From An Imaginary Western
4. Long Red
5. For Yasgur's Farm
6. You And Me

7. Waiting To Take You Away
8. Dreams Of Milk And Honey
9. Blind Man
10. Blue Suede Shoes
11. Southbound Train

Creedence Clearwater Revival

1. Born On The Bayou
2. Green River
3. Ninety-Nine And A Half
4. Commotion
5. Bootleg
6. Bad Moon Rising
7. Proud Mary
8. I Put A Spell On You
9. Night Time Is The Right Time
10. Keep On Choogin'
11. Suzy Q

Janis Joplin

1. Raise Your Hand
2. As Good As You've Been To This World
3. To Love Somebody
4. Summertime
5. Try (Just A Little Bit Harder)
6. Kosmic Blues
7. Can't Turn You Loose
8. Work Me Lord
9. Piece Of My Heart
10. Ball and Chain

Sly & The Family Stone

1. M'Lady
2. Sing A Simple Song
3. You Can Make It If You Try
4. Stand!
5. Love City
6. Dance To The Music
7. Music Lover
8. I Want To Take You Higher

The Who

1. Heaven And Hell
2. I Can't Explain
3. It's A Boy
4. 1921
5. Amazing Journey
6. Sparks
7. Eyesight To The Blind
8. Cristmas
9. Tommie Can You Hear Me
10. Acid Queen
11. Pinball Wizard
12. Abbie Hoffman Incident
13. Fiddle About
14. There's A Doctor I've Found
15. Go To The Mirror Boy
16. Smash The Mirror
17. I'm Free
18. Tommy's Holiday Camp
19. We're Not Gonna Take It
20. See Me Feel Me
21. Summertime Blues
22. Shakin' All Over

23. My Generation
24. Naked Eye

Jefferson Airplane

1. The Other Side Of This Life
2. Plastic Fantastic Lover
3. Volunteers
4. Saturday Afternoon / Won't You Try
5. Eskimo Blue Day
6. Uncle Sam's Blues
7. Somebody To Love
8. White Rabbit

Day Three: Sunday, August 17. 1969

Joe Cocker

1. Delta Lady
2. Some Things Goin' On
3. Let's Go Get Stoned
4. I Shall Be Released
5. With A Little Help From My Friends

Country Joe & The Fish
1. Barry's Caviar Dream
2. Not So Sweet Martha Lorraine
3. Rock And Soul Music
4. Thing Called Love
5. Love Machine
6. Fish Cheer / I-Feel-Like-I'm-Fixing-To-Die-Rag

Ten Years After

1. Good Morning Little Schoolgirl
2. I Can't Keep From Crying Sometimes
3. I May Be Wrong, But I Won't Be Wrong Always
4. I'm Going Home

The Band

1. Chest Fever
2. Don't Do It
3. Tears Of Rage
4. We Can Talk About It Now
5. Long Black Veil
6. Don't Ya Tell Henry
7. Ain't No More Cane on the Brazos
8. Wheels On Fire
9. Loving You Is Sweeter Than Ever
10. The Weight

Johnny Winter

1. Mama, Talk To Your Daughter
2. Leland Mississippi blues
3. Mean Town Blues
4. You've Done Lost Your Good Thing Now/Mean Mistreater
5. I Can't Stand It (with Edgar Winter)
6. Tobacco Road (with Edgar Winter)
7. Tell The Truth (with Edgar Winter)
8. Johnny B. Goode

Blood, Sweat and Tears

1. More and More
2. Just One Smile
3. Something Coming On

4. More Than You'll Ever Know
5. Spinning Wheel
6. Sometimes in Winter
7. Smiling Phases
8. God Bless The Child
9. I Stand Accused
10. And When I Die
11. You've Made Me So Very Happy

Crosby, Stills, Nash & Young

1. Suite Judy Blue Eyes
2. Blackbird
3. Helplessly Hoping
4. Guinnevere
5. Marrakesh Express
6. 4 + 20
7. Mr Soul
8. Wonderin'
9. You Don't Have To Cry
10. Pre-Road Downs
11. Long Time Gone
12. Bluebird Revisited
13. Sea Of Madness
14. Wooden Ships
15. Find The Cost Of Freedom
16. 49 Bye-Byes

Day Four: Monday, August 18. 1969

Paul Butterfield Blues Band

1. Everything's Gonna Be Alright
2. Driftin'
3. Born Under A Bad Sign
4. All My Love Comin' Through To You
5. Love March

Sha Na Na

1. Na Na Theme
2. Jakety Jak
3. Teen Angel
4. Jailhouse Rock
5. Wipe Out
6. Who Wrote The Book Of Love
7. Duke Of Earl
8. At The Hop
9. Na Na Theme

Jimi Hendrix

1. Message To Love
2. Getting My Heart Back Together Again
3. Spanish Castle Magic
4. Red House
5. Master Mind
6. Here Comes Your Lover Man
7. Foxy Lady
8. Beginning
9. Izabella
10. Gypsy Woman
11. Fire

12. Voodoo Child (Slight Return) / Stepping Stone
13. Star Spangled Banner
14. Purple Haze
15. Woodstock Improvisation / Villanova Junction
16. Hey Joe

Courtesy: DigitalDreamDoor.com

Author's note from Tom: In my research I discovered two different versions of the Woodstock lineup. I believe the reason for this is that one version represents the artists as they were *scheduled* to appear while the other version is the *actual* order of appearance. I attribute traffic and inclement weather to the schedule changes.

Woodstock RSVP: "No Thanks"

One can only wonder how Woodstock history, lore, albums and the movie would have been different had several acts not declined invitations to perform. Here are some of the more notable ones.

The Beatles: John Lennon said he couldn't get them together.

Led Zeppelin: The band got a higher-paying gig at the Asbury Park Convention Hall in New Jersey that weekend.

Bob Dylan: Turned it down because of his disgust of the hippies hanging around his Woodstock, New York house.

The Byrds: Turned it down because of a melee during their performance at the first Atlanta International Pop Festival held at the Atlanta International Raceway on July 4 and 5, 1969.

Tommy James and The Shondells: Turned it down because of being misinformed about the size and scope of the event.

Jethro Tull: Turned it down because they thought it wouldn't be a big deal.

The Moody Blues: They played a gig in Paris on that same weekend.

Courtesy: DigitalDreamDoor.com

"Sorry, We Gotta Cancel"

Not everyone who was supposed to perform at Woodstock performed at Woodstock. There were some cancellations. Here are four of the more notables.

Jeff Beck Group: The band had broken up in July, just a month before Woodstock, forcing cancellation.

Iron Butterfly: The band was stuck at the airport and their manager demanded helicopters and special arrangements just for them. Via Western Union they were not-so-politely told to "get lost."

Joni Mitchell: Joni's manager put her on the 'Dick Cavett Show' instead.

Lighthouse: (A Canadian band whose one-hit wonder was their 1971 *One Fine Morning*) Lighthouse feared it would be a "bad scene."

Courtesy: DigitalDreamDoor.com

PEOPLE MY AGE

ARE SO MUCH OLDER THAN ME

The Stories Behind The Music

We have finally come to the part of this book that first gave me the idea to do this book – The Stories Behind The Music.

Rod Stewart's song says, "Every picture tells a story." You're about to see that there's a story behind every song and band – stories you never knew!

In the introduction to this book I mentioned that I do a weekly feature called 'Z's School of Hard Rocks' on 105.7 WAPL-FM, in Appleton, Wisconsin. 'Z's School' was the brainchild of WAPL afternoon drive dee-jays Ryan 'Elwood' Bjorn and John Jordan who approached me with the idea in 2013.

At the time I had no idea it would soon have a cult-like following. I have been told by UPS drivers and even sheriffs deputies that they make sure their duties and routes find them in their vehicles at 4:10 every Friday afternoon when it's time for 'Z's School.'

The information for the stories that follow was gleaned from news reports, rock magazine articles, internet articles, fan websites and Wikipedia. These stories are merely snapshots and snippets of the much larger picture created by the artists and their songs.

'Z's School of Hard Rocks' is now in session!

"Keep playin, Richie! Keep playin'!"

Richie Havens will go down in rock and roll history as the performer who opened Woodstock on August 15, 1969. But actually, Havens was supposed to be the fifth act! Here's what happened.

There were massive traffic jams as thousands of concert-goers made their way to Yasgur's Farm and among those stuck in traffic were the scheduled openers as well as the acts that were to perform after Havens. Havens and his band took the stage at about 5pm and played their set. They were then called back for several encores as the highways were still at a virtual standstill. Havens ran out of songs to play and in desperation he improvised a song based upon the old spiritual *Motherless Child*. It is this song that we have come to know as *Freedom*.

The bottom line is the song that made it onto the Woodstock album and the song that catapulted Havens to stardom was made up on the spot! In an interview with Music-Room, Havens explained:

"I'd already played every song I knew and I was stalling, asking for more guitar and mic, trying to think of something else to play -- and then it just came to me...The establishment was foolish enough to give us all this freedom and we used it in every way we could."

Havens played for nearly 3 hours.

A Rough Beginning - Altamont

Rolling Stone Magazine called December 6, 1969 rock and roll's all-time worst day. Altamont.

The Altamont Speedway Free Festival was held in northern California between Tracy and Livermore. The headliners included Ike and Tina Turner, Santana, Jefferson Airplane, Crosby, Stills, Nash and Young and The Rolling Stones. It was just four months after Woodstock and the 300,000 people who attended Altamont thought it would be Woodstock West.

The vibes were bad from the start. There was violence, two hit-and-run deaths, a drowning in an irrigation canal, injuries, cars stolen and property damaged. Grace Slick said, "The vibes were bad. I had expected the loving vibes of Woodstock but that wasn't coming at me."

Seconds after getting out of his helicopter Mick Jagger was punched in the head by a concert-goer.

Security was provided by Hells Angels. Their fee was $500 worth of beer.

During the Rolling Stones set, 18-year-old Meredith Hunter rushed the stage and was beaten back by the Hells Angels. Meredith returned minutes later with a gun and one of the Angels stabbed him twice, killing him. Later, at trial, a self-defense argument resulted in a verdict of not guilty.

When the movie about Altamont called 'Gimme Shelter' came out the Hells Angels felt they had been negatively portrayed and blamed Jagger for his lack of support. In 2008 a former FBI agent claimed the Angels had hatched a plot to assassinate Jagger by using a boat to approach a residence where Jagger was staying on Long Island, New York. But a storm came up and the boat sank.

There is irony in the first line of the Stones' song *Gimme Shelter* as Jagger sings, "...a storm is threatening my very life today." In fact, it was a storm off Long Island that perhaps saved his life

Kissed By Bill Aucoin

William 'Bill' Aucoin takes his place in rock history as the manager of one of the most successful bands of all time.

Aucoin was born in 1943 and died in 2010 of prostate cancer. He was a Northwestern University graduate credited with discovering Kiss and managing them for a decade.

But while Aucoin hit the lottery with Kiss, he misjudged another band and will always be known as the manager who passed on a band called Van Halen.

While managing Kiss, Aucoin cut unheard-of business deals with the young band who had little business savvy. Aucoin got 25-percent of Kiss' tour, recording and merchandising revenues. Most other managers got 15-percent. Aucoin also owned the group's name and 50-percent of their publishing operations.

If a Kiss album cost $250,000 to produce, Aucoin was reportedly known to negotiate a $1 million advance, take $250,000 for himself and give the rest to the band to split among themselves.

The relationship between Aucoin and Kiss came to a halt in 1982 when the band wanted to go in a different direction. They were weary of their carnival-like routine and they wanted to get rid of the makeup. Aucoin vetoed the idea.

The band and Aucoin could not Kiss and makeup.

Black Betty

Ram Jam's 1977 hit *Black Betty* with its hard-driving guitar and edgy lyrics actually has a pretty softcore origin. Ram Jam's vocalist came from the Trans-Siberian Orchestra. Their bass player was with Billy Joel and their guitarist came from The Lemon Pipers who were one-hit wonders in 1967 with *Green Tambourine*.

Theories abound as to who or what Black Betty is.

One account holds that it is a rearrangement of Huddie Leadbelly Leadbetter's twentieth-century African-American work song of the same name, *Black Betty*.

Historically, Black Betty has served as a nickname for a number of objects – a musket, a bottle of whiskey, a whip or a prison transfer wagon.

In this observer's estimation, the evidence seems to point strongest to the musket theory. The "bam-a-lam" lyric perhaps refers to gunfire. The lyric, "Black Betty had a child" points to the child being the musket ball and "the damn thing gone wild" is the ball not always going where it should. The phrase, "the child is blind" could mean the musket ball didn't care who it hit, friend or foe. History tells us that in the Napoleonic /Russian War one-fourth of all casualties were caused by the rear ranks shooting their own.

Finally, "she's from Birmingham" could be a reference to Birmingham, Alabama where the muskets were produced.

There were those, however, who were convinced *Black Betty* was about a person which is why the NAACP and the Congress of Racial Equality called for a boycott of the song because of its lyrics.

Good Morning, Mr. Zappa!

Alice Cooper, born Vincent Furnier in Detroit, Michigan was the son of a preacher. Alice said he wrote many of his lyrics based upon the reaction to him by his mother's church group.

Following high school he and his band first called themselves The Earwigs and after that The Spiders. In 1967 they renamed themselves The Nazz until they learned The Nazz was already the name of Todd Rundgren's band. They went with the name Alice Cooper because the name sounded innocuous and wholesome in contrast to their image and stage act.

One night, after an unsuccessful gig at The Cheetah Club in Venice, California where they emptied the entire room in about ten minutes, a music manager named Shep Gordon approached them and said he knew of a guy who was looking to sign bizarre music acts to his new record label, Straight Records. That guy was Frank Zappa.

Zappa told the Alice Cooper band to come to his house at 7 o'clock to audition. The band mistakenly assumed Zappa meant 7 o'clock in the morning.

Being woken up by a band willing to play that brand of psychedelic music at 7 o'clock in the morning impressed Zappa enough to sign them to a three-record deal.

Eat A Peach For Peace

For all the great music the Allman Brothers Band produced, one would have thought that Howard Duane Allman enjoyed a long tenure with the band. But the fact is he was just 24 years old on that day when his motorcycle hit a flatbed truck in Macon, Georgia. Surgery could not save him.

Duane Allman was born in Nashville, Tennessee in 1947. His father was an army sergeant who was murdered by a soldier who was hitchhiking. The murder forced Duane's mother to retrain as an accountant and Duane and brother Gregg spent their summers at their grandmother's house in Nashville where they learned to play guitar.

They formed a band called The Escorts and even opened for The Beach Boys in 1965. Later they would change the band's name to the Allman Joys.

Duane became so proficient at playing guitar that in 2003 Rolling Stone Magazine listed him as the number two guitarist of all time only behind Jimi Hendrix.

Duane was a quick study. The story goes that in 1968 Duane got sick and brother Gregg dropped off a bottle of Coricidin cold medicine and a Taj Mahal album. An hour later, Gregg got a phone call from Duane. "Baby brother, baby brother, get over here, now!" When Gregg arrived he discovered that Duane had poured the pills out of the bottle, removed the label and did something he had never done before – played slide guitar using the bottle. He was doing a Taj Mahal cover called *Statesboro Blues*.

After Duane's death the band completed their latest album and named it for Duane's response to a question asked of him

by an interviewer – "How are you helping the revolution?"
Duane replied, "There ain't no revolution. Only evolution. But
everytime I'm in Georgia I eat a peach for peace."

No More Mr. Nice Guy

The song *No More Mr. Nice Guy* had personal meaning to Alice Cooper.

It was after young Vincent Furnier and his band entered their high school talent contest that they got the idea for using scare tactics and shock rock. This was a genre not looked upon kindly by the Christian community.

Vincent's father was a preacher and Vincent's mother was heavily involved in church activities.

His father's congregation began questioning him about his son's behavior and wondered why they should listen to anything he preached if his own son had turned demonic.

Vincent's mother's church group also had questions about Alice's stage performance and the characters he played.

Alice's response was that he "could have done a lot worse" with his life and "that's when the gloves came off."

Thus the lyrics in *No More Mr. Nice Guy*, "Mom's been thrown out of the social circles and dad has to hide."

And finally, the lyric that put Alice's dilemma into sharp focus. "I went to church incognito, when everybody rose, the Reverend Smith he recognized me and punched me in the nose. He said 'No more Mr. Nice Guy.'"

The Rooster

The Alice In Chains song *Rooster* is about a bird and Vietnam.

Alice In Chains' lead guitarist was Jerry Cantrell whose father served in Vietnam. Jerry's father would tell his son of the terrible things he had seen in Vietnam and what his homecoming was like. Thus, the lyrics:

"Walkin' tall, machine gun man. They spit on me in my homeland. Gloria sent me pictures of my boy. Got my pills against mosquito death. My buddy's breathin' his dyin' breath."

So where does the 'Rooster' fit into the picture? In Vietnam, the Marines carried a flag with an eagle on it. There were no eagles in Vietnam but the Vietnamese people were heavily into rooster farming. North Vietnamese soldiers thought the eagle was a rooster so each time they would stage an attack they would say, "It's time to snuff the rooster", in other words, time to kill the Americans.

When the song says, "Yeah, they've come to snuff the rooster. Oh, here comes the rooster. You know he ain't gonna die," it refers to Americans fighting back and surviving.

Whose Sweet Child Was He?

The pregnancy that resulted in William's birth was unplanned. William was just two years old when his father, also named William and known as a local delinquent, walked out on the family.

Young William's mother then married a man named Stephen Bailey and William took the name Bailey believing that Stephen Bailey was in fact, his biological father.

But later William would come to learn the truth and he hated his biological father so much that not only would he not take his last name, he no longer wanted to share his first name so he changed it to W. - W. Bailey.

Later, when W. Bailey got into rock and roll in Los Angeles his friends suggested that he get a first name. W. named himself after his favorite band - Axl.

At age 17 when Axl was going through some insurance papers at his parent's house he discovered his biological father's last name and for some reason re-adopted it. Rose.

Axl Rose would later learn what happened to the man who walked out on the family. William Rose, Sr. was murdered in Marion, Illinois in 1984 by an acquaintance. While the murderer was convicted, William Rose Sr.'s body was never found.

Hit Me With Your Best Guess

Patricia Mae Andrzejewski was born in Brooklyn, New York in 1953 to father Andrew who was a metal worker and mother Mildred who was a beautician.

Patricia was interested in theater and music and at an early age she performed in school plays, theater, parades and choirs. Her initial plans were to attend the Julliard School of Music, but to everyone's surprise she pursued a career in health education. She would marry her high school sweetheart and then worked as a bank teller outside Richmond, Virginia.

In 1973 she quit her bank teller job and pursued a singing career after being inspired by a Liza Minnelli concert.

Patricia would go on to win four Grammys for Best Female Rock Performance from 1980 to 1983. She is now a member of the Long Island Music Hall of Fame.

If you haven't yet figured out who Patricia Mae Andrzejewski is, take a guess. Hit Me With Your Best Shot.

Beck – Not Jeff

If you were to take a survey of music fans and ask them what they thought Kiss' biggest hit was, *Rock And Roll All Night* would probably be the answer given most frequently. They would be wrong.

Kiss had two gold-selling singles. Second place went to *I Was Made For Lovin' You*. The band's biggest single hit was *Beth*.

Beth was co-written by Kiss drummer Peter Criss and guitarist Stan Penridge prior to Criss joining Kiss. Criss and Penridge were in a band called Chelsea and the song was originally titled *Beck*. Beck was the nickname of fellow bandmember Mike Brand's wife Becky who would often call during practices to ask Mike when he was coming home.

When Criss joined Kiss and the band was working on the Destroyer album, Gene Simmons and Paul Stanley did not want *Beth* on the album, arguing it was not a typical Kiss song. Kiss' Manager Bill Aucoin insisted that the song be included and so it was.

As a single, *Beth* was the B-Side of *Detroit Rock City*. But the daughter of a Windsor, Ontario radio executive loved the song so much it became a radio hit to the point that Kiss presented the daughter with a gold record. The songs on the record were then flip-flopped and *Beth* became the A-Side.

The real irony of the song is that while it was Kiss' biggest hit in the band's history, not a single member of Kiss plays an instrument on the song. When it was recorded, the only person in the studio was Peter Criss who sang the song backed by a piano and a string orchestra.

Idolizing Billy

If someone were to ask you who would someday not only be one of the most famous punk rockers of all time, but also one of the first stars of MTV, the name William Albert Broad would probably not be your first answer.

William Albert Broad, born in England in 1955 is known to us by a different name thanks to one of his teachers who described him as 'idle'. Billy Idol.

Billy Idol's punk rock roots are deep and long. In 1976 he joined the punk rock band Siouxsie and the Banshees even before they had decided on that name. Later, he was the founder of the band Generation X.

Idol moved to New York City in 1981 where he teamed up with Kiss manager Bill Aucoin who played up Idol's glam rock bad boy image.

How cutting edge was he? What other self-respecting punk rocker would cover a Tommy James and The Shondells song -- *Mony Mony*? Idol did.

Idol almost added movie star to his credentials until he got into a serious motorcycle accident in Hollywood in 1990 that nearly cost him his leg. Movie director James Cameron had already chosen Idol to play the T-1000 character in 'Terminator 2 - Judgement Day' but the accident prevented Idol from taking the role.

Blackfoot

The southern rock band Blackfoot got their start in Jacksonville, Florida in 1970 when their original name was Fresh Garbage, a name they would later change to Hammer. At that time they relocated to Gainesville, Florida where they became the house band at Dub's, a well-known topless bar on the outskirts of town.

After a move to Manhattan in New York City they discovered there was a band on the west coast called Hammer so another name change was in the offing. Three of the band members were of American Indian heritage so they took on the name Blackfoot after the Blackfoot Tribe of Indians.

Blackfoot had two big hits, *Highway Song* and *Train Train*, a hard-driving song that logically would have come from the mind and guitar of lead guitarist and vocalist Rickey Medlocke.

But the song was actually written by Shorty Medlocke - Rickey's grandfather!

Blondie

Angela Tremble was born in Miami, Florida in July, 1945 and was adopted three months later by a family in Hawthorne, New Jersey.

In 1980 she held jobs as a beautician, barmaid and Playboy bunny and in 1981 Harpers Bazaar Magazine named her to their '10 Most Beautiful Women In America' list.

In the mid-seventies she had formed a band called Angel and The Snake. However, they changed the name after truck drivers would call to her, "Hey, Blondie!" as she walked down the street. The band had a new name - Blondie. Angela Tremble, nicknamed Blondie and also known as Debbie would be the frontwoman for Blondie.

Beside her role as musician she is also ranked number 12 on VH1's 'Greatest Women of Rock and Roll.' She once worked in one of New York City's very first head shops, a shop specializing in drug paraphernalia. She was also a good friend of Nancy Spungen, the girlfriend of punk rock musician Sid Vicious.

 Asked about her refusal to locate her birth parents, Debbie reportedly said, "I know who I am and it would be an insult to the Harrys."

The Harry's adopted the little girl who would become Debra Harry.

Blue On Black

Kenny Wayne Shepherd's 1998 hit *Blue On Black* was number one that year on Billboard Magazine's Hot Mainstream Rock Tracks and was regarded by various media as the best rock song of 1998.

But what were the somber lyrics and haunting guitar riffs all about?

It would appear the narrator had just been through a tough breakup and there was heartbreak and regret involved. Worst of all, he can't change it. There is nothing he can do about it and it all means nothing. Thus the lyrics:

Blue on black,
tears on a river,
push on a shove,
it don't mean much.

Joker on jack,
match on a fire,
cold on ice,
a dead man's touch.

Whisper on a scream,
doesn't change a thing,
doesn't bring you back.

Blue on black.

Don't Fear The Aliens

Their manager Sandy Pearlman saw his Long Island, New York band as America's answer to Black Sabbath.

It was Pearlman who gave the band its name -- Soft White Underbelly. The name came from a phrase used by Winston Churchill in describing Italy during World War II.

After a time, Pearlman decided it was time for another name change. And while the band did not like this new name, they settled for it because they were getting ready to record their first release.

This new name came from some poetry Pearlman had written. In one of his poems he wrote about a group of aliens who had assembled secretly to guide earth's history.

These aliens called themselves The Blue Oyster Cult.

Bon Scott

Ronald Belford Scott - Bon Scott - was the lead singer of the Australian hard rock band ACDC from 1974 until his death in 1980.

In the July, 2004 issue of Classic Rock Magazine, Scott was number one on the list of the '100 Greatest Frontmen of All Time' ahead of Freddie Mercury and Robert Plant.

Bon Scott was just 33 years old on the night of February 19, 1980 when he passed out after a night of heavy drinking in a London Club called The Music Machine. He was left to sleep in a Renault-5 owned by an acquaintance named Alistair Kinnear.

The following afternoon, Kinnear found Scott lifeless and Scott was pronounced dead-on-arrival at King's College Hospital. Initial speculation was that the cause of death was 'aspiration of vomit'. But the official death certificate says 'death by acute alcohol poisoning' and classified as 'death by misadventure'.

Bon Scott's gravesite has become a cultural landmark. The National Trust of Australia decreed his grave to be important enough to be included on the list of Classified Heritage Places. At this writing, Bon Scott's grave is reportedly the most visited grave in all of Australia.

Brian Jones

He should be enjoying life as the founder and original bandleader of the most enduring rock and roll band in history. Unfortunately, he has been in a coffin for nearly 50 years.

Lewis Brian Hopkins Jones, better known to us as Brian Jones was born in England in 1942. A bout with the croup at age four left him with asthma for the rest of his life.

Jones was said to be a genius who had an IQ of 135, a student who never studied but aced all of his exams. Said one childhood friend, he was a rebel without a cause, but when it came to examinations he was brilliant.

Jones had four children with four different women. His first child was born in 1960 and was given up for adoption which means there is someone out there between the ages of 50 and 60 who probably has no idea that he or she is the child of Brian Jones.

One of the other four children was the result of a one night stand with a married woman. Jones never knew of that birth.

The birth of the Rolling Stones occurred when Jones took out an ad in a tabloid looking for members to form a band. Mick Jagger and childhood friend Keith Richards responded. When they formed their band they received a call from a club owner looking to book them and the club owner asked, "What are you called?" The band had no name. Lying on the floor was a Muddy Waters album and side one, track five was *Rollin' Stone*.

Drugs and alcohol turned Jones anti-social and he rarely associated with his bandmates. His role in the band diminished and in 1969 he was asked to leave. One month later he was found dead at the bottom of his swimming pool. The coroner's report noted his heart and liver were enlarged due to alcohol and drug abuse.

Jones is buried in his hometown of Cheltenham. Instead of the normal depth of 6 feet, Jones' coffin is buried 12 feet down to guard against exhumation by trophy hunters.

Tears In Heaven

His name was Conor and at this writing he would be about 30 years old had it not been for that fateful day of March 20, 1991.

On that day Conor was with his mother Lory Del Santo and a nanny in their 53rd floor New York City apartment. Conor wanted to play hide and seek. He ran and the nanny chased him. The nanny was stopped momentarily by a maintenance worker who told her he had just slid open a floor-to-ceiling window. In that split second, Conor ran through the window and fell 49 stories, landing on the roof of a four-story building below.

Lory was stunned and collapsed. Dad came home five minutes later not realizing his son had fallen out of the window. Lory screamed, "He's dead." Dad's eyes went dark and he said, "Dead. He's dead. It's impossible."

Dad dealt with the horrible tragedy in the only way he knew how. He wrote a song, the first line of which says, "Would you know my name, if I saw you in Heaven?"

Conor was Conor Clapton. His dad's name is Eric.

Summertime Blues

The song *Summertime Blues* was written by Eddie Cochran, a man who seemed to be eerily surrounded by death.

Born in Minnesota in 1938, Cochran's style of music would come to be known as Rockabilly. *Summertime Blues* was his biggest hit and reached number 73 on Billboard Magazine's Greatest Hits of All Time list. He was inducted into the Rock and Roll Hall of Fame in 1987.

Summertime Blues has been covered by bands like Blue Cheer and most notably The Who.

Eddie Cochran's first encounter with death was in 1959 when two of his close friends, Buddy Holly and Richie Valens along with the Big Bopper died in a plane crash. Cochran was shaken by their deaths and he developed a morbid premonition that he too would die young. In fact, he wanted to give up life on the road to reduce the chance of suffering a similar fatal accident. But Cochran had a family and financial responsibilities so he accepted an offer to do a United Kingdom tour in 1960.

On Saturday, April 16th while on that tour Cochran was killed when a speeding taxi he was in crashed. He was in the middle seat and was thrown out of the car after he reportedly threw himself over his fiancé. Along with Cochran in that taxi was his Gretsch guitar.

Earlier on that tour, a 12-year-old boy named Mark Feld carried that Gretsch guitar for Cochran to Cochran's waiting car. Young Mark was obviously influenced by Cochran because he would later form his own band and do his own cover of *Summertime Blues*.

Young Mark would die 17 years later in a 1977 car crash in southwest London. He too was a passenger. At 12 years old he was Mark Feld. We would come to know him as Marc Bolan of T-Rex.

Copperhead Road

Steve Earle's *Copperhead Road* is the tale of three generations running contraband goods and also adds some irony and history into the mix.

The song is sung by a young man who carries the name of his father and grandfather - John Lee Pettimore. His grandfather was a rum runner in Tennessee as noted in the lyric: "You hardly ever saw Grandaddy down here. He only came to town about twice a year. He'd buy a hundred pounds of yeast and some copper line. Everybody knew that he made moonshine." And pity the federal tax agent who tried to bring Grandaddy down: "Now the revenue man wanted Grandad bad. He headed up the holler with everything he had. 'Fore my time but I've been told. He never come back from Copperhead Road."

John Lee's father carried on the operation Grandaddy started. Ironically, the rum running operation was facilitated by an old sheriff's car that dad bought at a Mason's Lodge auction. He painted it and modified the engine so he could outrun the sheriff who showed up in the middle of the night as dad "headed down to Knoxville with the weekly load. You could smell the whiskey burnin' down Copperhead Road."

Young John Lee joined the Army and did two tours of Vietnam where he learned two things from Charlie (the name the Americans gave to the Viet Cong soldiers). The first was how to grow seeds to produce illegal drugs. "I take the seed from Columbia and Mexico. I just plant it up the holler down Copperhead Road." Was the second lesson learned from Charlie the how-to of taking down helicopters - as in Drug Enforcement Agency helicopters?

57

"And now the D.E.A's got a chopper in the air. I wake up screaming like I'm back over there. I learned a thing or two from Charlie don't you know. You better stay away from Copperhead Road."

Ded Flatbird

The band formed in Sheffield, England in 1977 and performed under the name Atomic Mass. Who could have guessed that by 1983 their new name would be a household name when their hit single *Photograph* replaced Michael Jackson's *Beat It* as the most requested videoclip on MTV.

Def Leppard would go on to sell 100 million albums worldwide.

The name Def Leppard was the brainchild of one of the band members who would dream up imaginary band names during English class. He said the name was, at least in part, a takeoff of Led Zeppelin.

On New Years Eve, 1984 drummer Rick Allen lost his arm in a car crash in Sheffield. Thanks to the use of his legs and an electronic drum kit he was able to continue performing with the band.

Def Leppard played Las Vegas' Hard Rock Hotel and Casino in March and April of 2013 and the band that opened for them billed itself as the world's best Def Leppard coverband. This coverband would play all the songs that Def Leppard did not usually play in concert.

This coverband performed under the name Ded Flatbird and they lived up to their billing. They really were the best Def Leppard coverband in the world.

Ded Flatbird was, in fact, Def Leppard. Def Leppard opened for themselves!

Dio

Ronald James Padavona was born in Cortland, New York in 1942 and took a roundabout route to a rock career that spanned 50 years.

He learned to play the trumpet at age 5 and was influenced vocally by opera tenor Mario Lanza. After high school Padavona turned down a scholarship to the prestigious Julliard School of Music because of his interest in rock and roll. Instead, he enrolled in pharmacology school at the University of Buffalo.

He would go on to front several bands including Elf, Rainbow, Black Sabbath, Heaven and Hell and his own band - Dio. Ronald James Padavona was Ronnie James Dio.

Dio was diagnosed with stomach cancer causing Heaven and Hell to cancel all of their summer dates that year. Despite Dio's intention to make it back to the stage, it never happened and he died on May 16, 2010.

His unmistakable, though untrained voice lives on. He claimed to never have had any vocal training and attributed his singing ability to the use of correct breathing techniques he learned while playing the trumpet.

Ah, Leah!

Dominic Ierace, born in New Castle, Pennsylvania in February, 1948 would come to be known as Donnie Iris, best known for his hit song, *Ah, Leah!*

The song was born in Iris' basement when Donnie and a friend were trying to come up with an anti-war song. They came up with a war chant, Ahleah! Ahleah! Ahleah! But Iris felt that this war chant sounded more like a girl's name, so the war chant became a love song instead.

At first glance it would appear that Donnie Iris was a one hit wonder. But he played a part in two other songs near and dear to the hearts of old rockers. Iris' first band was The Jaggerz who had a 1970 hit with *The Rapper*. Later, he was with a band called Wild Cherry which will go down in rock history for their *Play That Funky Music, White Boy.*

Meditating About the Doors

Doors co-founder and keyboardist Ray Manzarek was 74 when he died of bile duct cancer in Rosenheim, Germany in 2013.

Had it not been for basketball and a man named Yogi, we may have never heard of Ray Manzarek.

Manzarek grew up on the south side of Chicago where he was an avid basketball player playing the positions of center or power forward. So when his high school coach insisted he play guard or not at all, Manzarek quit the team. Manzarek said had it not been for that ultimatum he might never have been with the Doors.

Rather than play college basketball, Manzerek went to film school at UCLA where he met Jim Morrison. Morrison showed Manzarek a few songs he had written and he sang a rough version of *Moonlight Drive.* Manzarek liked the songs and the Doors became a reality.

Drummer John Densmore and guitarist Robbie Krieger came to join the band in a most unusual fashion. Manzarek met them at a Transcendental Meditation lecture. Said Densmore, "There wouldn't be any Doors without Maharishi Mahesh Yogi."

Kiss And the Three Stooges

Kiss' *Calling Doctor Love* on their 1976 Rock And Roll Over album was the band's fourth top-twenty single and got as high as number 16 on the Billboard chart. A live version of the song appears on the 1977 Kiss Alive II album.

The song was written by Kiss bassist and lead vocalist Gene Simmons who wrote it in the most unlikely of places -- a Holiday Inn in Evansville, Indiana.

The idea for *Calling Doctor Love* came when Simmons thought back to a Three Stooges film called Men in Black which contained the hospital-scene announcement, "Calling Dr. Howard, Dr. Fine, Dr. Howard."

The Power Of Ed

It was Ed Sullivan who introduced America to the Beatles on that Sunday night in February, 1964.

In subsequent weeks he would introduce us to The Dave Clark Five, The Rolling Stones, Herman's Hermits, Freddie and The Dreamers and many others.

On January 15, 1967, the Rolling Stones were making their fourth appearance on the show and they were scheduled to do a song called *Let's Spend the Night Together*. Sullivan objected and ordered the band to change the lyrics. Sullivan felt America was not ready for a song about a male and female spending the 'night' together and suggested the word be changed to 'time'.

Dutifully, the band sang the song with the word 'time' although Mick Jagger rolled his eyes each time he said the word just to let his teenage audience know it wasn't his idea. Midway through the song he was able to slip in one 'night'.

The Rolling Stones weren't the only ones to feel Sullivan's wrath. In 1963 Sullivan told Bob Dylan he could not perform his song, *Talkin' John Birch Paranoid Blues* and asked Dylan to pick a different song. Dylan refused and walked out.

When the Doors wanted to perform *Light My Fire* on the show, Sullivan told them to take out the ever-so-offensive word 'higher' claiming the word had a drug connotation. Unlike Jagger, Jim Morrison did not roll his eyes or give in and the Doors were banned from the program.

Elvin Bishop

Elvin Bishop is best known for his 1976 *Fooled Around And Fell In Love*. But few of us know of the horrific murder that touched his life.

Elvin Bishop was born in 1942 in Glendale, California. He grew up on a farm in Iowa and later moved to Oklahoma. It was at Will Rogers High School in Oklahoma that he won a full scholarship to the University of Chicago as a National Merit Scholar finalist.

While majoring in physics at the University of Chicago he met Paul Butterfield and joined the Paul Butterfield Blues Band for five years. Bishop would later go on to play with Mike Bloomfield and Al Kooper.

For as well as we know the song *Fooled Around And Fell In Love*, most people don't realize that Elvin Bishop was not the vocalist. The song was sung by Mickey Thomas who would later join Jefferson Starship.

Bishop was even known to sit in with the Greatful Dead. It was the dead who would figure into another important event in his life. Not the Greatful Dead. The dead.

In August, 2000 in California, Bishop's 45-year-old ex-wife Jenifer Villarin and a man named James Gamble were found shot to death. Villarin had been house sitting for their 22-year-old daughter Salina. Four days later, Salina's body was found in several duffle bags in the Mokelumne River.

The murders were the result of an elaborate scheme to extort $100,000 from an elderly couple. Two men were convicted and sentenced to death. One committed suicide in San Quentin Prison.

Eruption

Eddie Van Halen's guitar solo *Eruption* precedes the band's cover of the Kinks' *You Really Got Me*.

It may surprise you to know that *Eruption* almost didn't make it onto the 1978 Van Halen debut album. In fact, we may have never heard of *Eruption* had it not been for a twist of fate.

Eddie was warming up at the recording studio early one day when producer Ted Templeman overheard the guitarist playing a solo. Templeman loved what he heard and demanded that they record the solo. Eddie quickly recorded one take of *Eruption* and they put it on the album.

According to Eddie, "I didn't even play it right. There's a mistake at the top of it. To this day whenever I hear it I always think, man I could've played that better."

David Essex

David Albert Cook was born in 1947 in Plaistow, London to a dockworker father and a mother who was a self-employed pianist.

He would become known not just for his music but for his acting and writing abilities as well. He appeared in Godspell, various television shows and in musicals.

We know David Albert Cook for his 1974 hit single *Rock On*, the song that sold one million copies and resulted in David being voted the number one British male vocalist that year. David Albert Cook is David Essex.

But for all of his accomplishments, we almost never heard of him. David wanted to be a professional soccer player and even reached semi-professional status. In fact, he purposely failed a test required to get into grammar school so that he would have to attend a nearby secondary school that had a soccer team.

As for the meaning of *Rock On*, one lyric in particular may give us a clue. "Where do we go from here? Which is the way that's clear?" In the 1950's, U.S. artists dominated the music scene. *Rock On* refers to the time British musicians began to believe they too, could write rock music and started to create their own style.

History has proven they were correct.

Locomotion

She went by the stage name Little Eva. Eva Narcissus Boyd was born June 29, 1943 in Belhaven, North Carolina and died April 10, 2003. How could this little girl know that someday she would be musically connected to the likes of Grand Funk Railroad and Todd Rundgren?

Eva worked in New York as a maid and babysitter for singer-songwriter Carol King and husband Gerry Goffin. Carol heard Eva sing and knew one day the young lady would make it big. Eva did make it big with a song that Carol King sang backup on. The song would wind up as number 359 on Billboard Magazine's 500 Greatest Songs of All Time. That song was the 1962 hit *Locomotion*.

The song was covered by Grand Funk Railroad when producer Todd Rundgren heard GFR's lead guitarist Mark Farner whistling it in the studio and the band decided to do it.

When Little Eva died at the age of 59 of cervical cancer in Kinston, North Carolina, she was buried in a deteriorating cemetery in her hometown of Belhaven. The cemetery caught the attention of a local television station and improvements were made. The simple white cross that marked Eva's resting place was replaced by a new, gray headstone. Prominently engraved on the headstone is an epitaph that reads, "Singing With The Angels."

What is also engraved on the front of the headstone is the image of a steam locomotive.

Signs

The original version of *Signs* was released in 1971 by The Five Man Electrical Band. Nearly 20 years later, Tesla did a cover version in 1990.

The Five Man Electrical Band began in 1963 as the Staccatos in Ottawa, Canada. Although they co-recorded an album with fellow Canadian rockers The Guess Who, international success eluded them.

Signs had its origin when guitarist Les Emmerson was driving along Route 66 in California and noticed that a number of billboards were obscuring his view. He saw that as a perfect metaphor for the frustration of the band.

Signs was originally the B-Side of a record called *Hello Melinda Goodbye* which failed miserably and caused the band to return home to plan an uncertain future. But a record promoter suggested that the group make *Signs* the A-Side of the record and when they did the song took off on Billboard Magazine's Hot 100 chart, sold one million copies and went gold.

The result was the band ended up sharing the stage with such major acts as the Allman Brothers, Sly and the Family Stone and Jefferson Airplane. They are now among other Canadian rock legends that include The Stampeders of *Time Won't Let Me* fame, April Wine, Bachman-Turner Overdrive and The Guess Who.

Gimme Three Steps

Lynyrd Skynyrd's *Gimme Three Steps* wasn't just a song. It really happened!

The band's debut album in 1973 contained *Gimme Three Steps* but the song never charted. The album's success was attributed instead to *Free Bird*.

Gimme Three Steps tells the story of a man who was dancing in a bar with a girl named Linda Lou when the woman's jealous boyfriend enters and threatens the man with a gun. The man asks the jealous boyfriend, "Gimme three steps" so he would have time to flee.

The incident actually happened to band member Ronnie Van Zant at a biker bar known as the Pastime in Jacksonville, Florida where he had a gun pulled on him. That night on the way home he wrote the lyrics to *Gimme Three Steps*.

The lyric that says "Wait a minute mister, I didn't even kiss her" got changed after the plane crash that killed some of the band members and Ronnie and Johnny Van Zant reformed the band. The change appeared not on the album but rather in the band's live concerts where they would sing, "Wait a minute mister, I didn't even stick her."

Radar Love

It was 1961 in The Hague, Netherlands when a 13-year-old boy and his 15-year-old neighbor formed a band which would eventually stand the test of time along with the likes of the Rolling Stones and the Beach Boys as one of the longest-performing acts in music history.

The boys called themselves the Tornados until they discovered the name was being used by another band. Their new name was taken from the title of a song done by the British group The Hunters for whom they sometimes opened and closed. The name of the song was Golden Earring.

Between 1969 and 1984 Golden Earring opened for such acts as Santana, King Crimson, the Doobie Brothers, Rush and 38 Special. In 1973 and '74 when their song *Radar Love* became a huge hit bands like Kiss and Aerosmith opened for them!

Golden Earring's sound was influenced by acts like Jimi Hendrix, Led Zeppelin, Procol Harum and Eric Clapton.

On stage they were loud and powerful. What made them that way was the fact that for their concerts they rented the superb quadraphonic sound system normally used exclusively by The Who.

Grand Funk Railroad

While the critics hated them, audiences loved them and Rolling Stone Magazine said you cannot talk about rock in the 70's without talking about this band.

The band's hometown was Flint, Michigan through which the Grand Trunk Western Railroad ran. With a little play on words they came up with the name Grand Funk Railroad. Their leader was singer/guitarist Mark Farner. Don Brewer played drums and the bass player Mel Schachner came from Question Mark and the Mysterians of *96 Tears* fame.

In 1970 Grand Funk Railroad sold more albums than any other American band and in 1971 they broke the Beatles' Shea Stadium attendance record by selling the place out in just 72 hours.

The band always sought to improve themselves to the point that had he not been committed to a record deal, none other than Peter Frampton was going to join them. GFR's songs *We're An American Band* and *Locomotion* were produced by rock legend Todd Rundgren and later they would be produced by Frank Zappa.

Heart

You might say that two of Heart's biggest hits had their roots in anger.

Heart, fronted by sisters Ann and Nancy Wilson has sold more than 30-million albums in its more than four-decade run and the band has taken its place in the Rock and Roll Hall of Fame.

It is reported that in 1977 in a contract dispute Heart parted company with Mushroom Records where they were working on the Magazine album. They signed with Portrait Records and got to work on *Little Queenie*. Heart and the two record companies got into a nasty legal battle which gave birth to the song *Heartless*.

Also in 1977 Mushroom Records ran a full-page ad in Rolling Stone Magazine showing the bare-shouldered Wilson sisters posing much like they did on the Dreamboat Annie album cover with a suggestive caption that said, "It was only our first time." When a reporter suggested backstage after a live performance that the sisters were sex partners, the infuriated Ann returned to her hotel room and began writing the lyrics to *Barricuda*.

Happy Trails, Woodstock

Jimi Hendrix closed Woodstock with a two-hour set, one of the longest of his career. The set will always be remembered for Hendrix' version of *The Star Spangled Banner,* but it should be remembered that the national anthem was just part of a medley that included *Voodoo Chile* and *Purple Haze.*

Contrary to popular belief, it wasn't the Jimi Hendrix Experience performing but instead a group Hendrix assembled called Gypsy Suns and Rainbows. The Experience had broken up two summers earlier.

Hendrix was supposed to perform Sunday night, but bad weather pushed Hendrix' set to Monday morning at 9, his only major morning performance. The benefit of the morning performance was that the morning sun made for excellent filming conditions which is part of the reason the performance is so well-known.

Unique about this performance was the fact that Hendrix did something he rarely did -an encore. History shows that the encore was *Hey Joe,* but before he came out on stage for the encore, Hendrix was heard talking about doing a song called *Valleys of Neptune* instead.

Ironically, Jimi Hendrix was not supposed to be the closing act at Woodstock. Woodstock organizer Michael Lang wanted another act to come on after Hendrix. Let the history books show that Roy Rogers declined the invitation to close Woodstock with *Happy Trails.*

Here's Some News!

Hugh Anthony Gregg was born in New York City in 1950 to a Boston doctor father and a Polish immigrant mother.

Hugh was of such high intelligence that not only did he skip second grade, but at Lawrenceville High School in New Jersey he got a perfect score of 800 on the math portion of the S.A.T. At Cornell University he would major in engineering. It really was *Hip to Be Square*. Hugh Anthony Gregg would come to be known to us as Huey Lewis.

Before college he hitchhiked around the world, learning to play harmonica as he waited for rides.

Later, his band would open for Van Morrison and under the name Huey Harp he played on Thin Lizzy's landmark album Live and Dangerous.

A movie would land Lewis in court. He filed suit against Ray Parker Junior who wrote the theme song for the movie Ghostbusters. Lewis contended that the song was much too similar to his *I Want A New Drug* and the case was settled out of court.

We're Not Pretending

Chrissie Hynde of The Pretenders came from humble beginnings in Akron, Ohio where her father was a Yellow Pages Manager and her mother was a part-time secretary.

Her connection to history - she attended Kent State University and was on campus on the day of the Kent State shootings on May 4, 1970.

Later, she would move to London to work for a music magazine and at a little-known clothing store called SEX. In an attempt to get a work permit she tried to get a guy who hung out at the store to marry her. That guy was Sid Vicious.

Hynde's early musical career found her with a band called the Moors Murderers in 1978 - a band named after two child killers. Later, the band would become the Pretenders, a name based upon The Platters 1955 hit *The Great Pretender*. The Pretenders entered the Rock and Roll Hall of Fame in 2005.

Beside her career with The Pretenders, Hynde performed a duet with Frank Sinatra in 1994. The duo did *Luck Be A Lady*.

In 2007 Hynde opened a vegan restaurant in Akron, Ohio that was voted one of the top five vegan restaurants in the United States.

Hynde has a daughter with Ray Davies of the Kinks.

Decisions That Changed History

November 22, 1963 aboard Air Force One. Vice President Lyndon Johnson was about to be sworn in as President of the United States just hours after the assassination of President John F. Kennedy. Johnson asked that First Lady Jacqueline Kennedy be present for the swearing-in. Other historical accounts claim Jackie was at the back of the plane when she was informed that the swearing-in was about to happen She was told she need not attend but she insisted. Johnson's wife, Lady Bird asked Jackie if she would like to change out of her blood-stained dress to which Jackie replied, "No, let them see what they have done to him."

How different history would have looked had Jackie not made that decision. To this day we can still see the black and white photograph of Johnson's raised right hand and Jackie standing next to him in that blood-stained dress.

Fast forward seven years from that day as Black Sabbath was about to release their album Paranoid. One of the cuts on the album was *Iron Man*, a song about a man who time travels into the future and in the process of returning he is turned into steel by a magnetic field and is rendered mute. He tries to warn everyone of an impending apocalypse but his attempts to communicate are ignored and mocked. He becomes angry and takes his revenge out on mankind and causes destruction.

When Ozzy Osbourne first heard the song he said it sounded, "Like a big iron bloke walking about."

How different would music history have been had Ozzy's suggestion for a title come to pass. *Iron Man* would have been *Iron Bloke*.

In A Gadda Da Vida

Iron Butterfly's *In A Gadda Da Vida*, the 17-minute rock anthem has a place in music history because it marked the early transition from psychedelic music to heavy metal. Joining in the movement were groups like Blue Cheer, The Jimi Hendrix Experience and Steppenwolf.

There are a few different versions of just how the song got its name. One story goes that the original title was *In The Garden of Eden* but that during rehearsal singer Doug Ingle was so drunk he slurred the words, creating what stuck as the title.

Another version says drummer John Bushy was listening through headphones and couldn't clearly distinguish what Ingle was singing.

A third version says Ingle was drunk and high and when Ingle was told the name of the song he wrote it down incorrectly.

Iron Butterfly would have become a part of Woodstock history had they not been stuck at the airport. Their manager reportedly demanded of Woodstock's promoters that a helicopter be sent for the band, the band would do their set, be paid and be flown back to the airport.

The promoter never called back. The helicopter never came.

Isle of Wight

It was the festival that gave birth to all the other festivals - The Isle of Wight in Afton Down, England in 1968 through 1970 and revived in 2002.

It was the 1970 event where rock history was made. That year's lineup was enough to make a Woodstock fan jealous -- The Who, Jimi Hendrix, Ten Years After, The Doors, Emerson, Lake and Palmer, Joni Mitchell, the Moody Blues, Melanie, Donovan, Chicago, Richie Havens, John Sebastian, Jethro Tull, Taste and even Tiny Tim.

600,000 people congregated on the tiny island, a crowd so large that it led to the British Parliament passing the Isle of Wight Act in 1971 which prohibited gatherings of 5000 people or more on the island without a license.

To grasp the import of this event consider the fact that when the Woodstock Festival was being held in Bethel, New York, it was assumed that Bethel's (actually Woodstock's) most famous resident would play there - Bob Dylan. But on August 15, the day Woodstock opened, Dylan left Bethel for the Isle of Wight.

The James Gang

The hard rock band formed in Cleveland, Ohio in 1962 who we've come to know as The James Gang actually had its roots in Top-40 and even Bubblegum!

The band's drummer was once with a Cleveland-area band called The Outsiders who were one-hit-wonders with the 1965 hit *Time Won't Let Me.*

In 1968 The James Gang hired a manager away from The Lemon Pipers who had just scored with their one-hit-wonder song *My Green Tambourine.*

The band was named after an 1800's gang of outlaws and went through a series of guitarists until a guitarist named Joe Walsh asked for an audition and the rest is history.

They opened for the Who on the Who's 1970 tour and shared the stage with such acts as Grand Funk Railroad, The Kinks, Humble Pie, Three Dog Night and Led Zeppelin.

The James Gang sometimes had five members and sometimes four. But there was that one night in Detroit when the James Gang was almost no more. It was just before they were about to go on stage at the Motown Grand Ballroom to open for Cream when guitarist Ronnie Silverman informed Walsh and the other two that he wasn't going on.

The other three band members, in desperate need of money, went on stage as a trio, liked their sound and decided to remain a trio.

The Night Janis Died

Janis Joplin died at Hollywood's Landmark Hotel on October 4, 1970. Earlier that evening she had gone out for drinks, came back to her hotel room and shot up her last fix of heroin. She went downstairs to the hotel lobby to get change for a five-dollar bill so she could buy some cigarettes, chatted with the hotel clerk and went back to her room where she collapsed and died - cigarette in hand.

The 27-year-old Joplin had been in L.A. for the recording of her last album, Pearl. The only song she hadn't finished was *Buried Alive In the Blues.*

Happier times for Janis Joplin were had at Woodstock where she did alcohol and heroin during her 10-hour backstage wait before her performance. After her set she stayed for the rest of the festival and was said to have particularly enjoyed Sly and the Family Stone who played right after her.

Joplin was also there to witness Jimi Hendrix closing the show. She was with Joan Baez and they watched it from Joe Cocker's van.

Jethro Tull

To tell the story of Jethro Tull is to tell the story of two farmers.

The first farmer was born in Basildon, Berkshire England in 1674. He would revolutionize British farming by inventing a horse-drawn seed drill that economically planted seeds in the ground. Farmers no longer had to plant one seed at a time. His name was Jethro Tull.

The second farmer is a salmon farmer, Mr. Anderson by name. At this writing Mr. Anderson employed 400 people on his salmon farm in Straithaird, Scotland. The farm was the largest independent smoked salmon producer in the United Kingdom. This farmer's name is Ian Anderson, leader of the band Jethro Tull.

Just as farmer Tull revolutionized farming, farmer Anderson revolutionized rock music as the first big name rock musician to play the flute.

Joan of Rock

Joan Marie Larkin, born in Philadelphia in 1958 would become a founding member of the 70's bad-girl band The Runaways alongside drummer Sandy West, Jackie Fox, Cherie Currie and Lita Ford. The band opened for such acts as Cheap Trick, The Ramones, Van Halen and Tom Petty and The Heartbreakers.

In her post-Runaways days the press touted Joan as 'The Godmother of Punk'. Mattel even produced a Joan Jett Barbie doll in 2009.

Joan's favorite guitar was her white Melody Maker that she bought from Eric Carmen following the breakup of The Raspberries.

Joan has a couple of notable sports connections to her credit. First, at Cal Ripkin Junior's request, Joan sang the National Anthem at the Baltimore Orioles game in which Ripkin tied Lou Gehrig's record for consecutive games played.

And as every NFL fan knows, the melody for her song *I Hate Myself For Lovin' You* was used as the theme for NBC's Sunday Night Football with reworked lyrics and retitled *Waiting All Day For Sunday Night*.

Juke Box Hero

Foreigner's song *Juke Box Hero* has its roots in reality.

Juke Box Hero tells the story of a boy who was unable to purchase a ticket to a sold-out rock concert. From outside the concert hall he hears one of the guitars, he has an epiphany, buys a guitar and without the aid of lessons he becomes famous.

Juke Box Hero was written by Foreigner lead guitarist Mick Jones and lead singer Lou Graham. To quote Jones, "We'd gone to the arena (Cincinnati's Riverfront Stadium) for a sound check and it was pouring down rain and there were a bunch of fans waiting at the door when we went in. When we came back for the show later on all that was left was one lonely fan, a young guy waiting out there in the rain, soaked to the skin. I thought, well, he's waiting like five hours here - maybe we take him in and give him a glimpse of what happens backstage at a show. And this kid was just mesmerized with everything. I saw the look in his eyes and I thought he's seeing this for the first time - he's having this experience."

The Kinks and Coca Cola

In his autobiography, Kinks lead singer Ray Davies admitted he was aiming for a hit when he wrote the song *Lola*. Said Davies, "Something that would sell in the first five seconds."

The song did become a hit but not before it was almost banned and not before Davies made two trans-Atlantic flights to keep it from being banned.

Lola is a tongue-in-cheek tale of infatuation between a hapless young man and the transvestite who steals his heart.

On the eve of the single's release the Kinks got word that the BBC wouldn't play it because of a lyric about drinking champagne that tastes like Coca Cola which went against the BBC's product placement policy. The Kinks were on tour in the U.S. at the time, so after the May 23rd show in Minnesota, Davies flew back to Great Britain and recorded several overdubs changing Coca Cola to cherry cola. But despite his best efforts, Davies was not satisfied with the track.

Davies flew back to the U.S. to make it to a show in Chicago, then flew back to London and gave the redub another shot which was finally successful and the song passed BBC muster.

LaGrange

ZZ Top's *LaGrange*, released as a single in 1973, ranks number 74 in Rolling Stone Magazine's list of the 100 Greatest Guitar Songs of All Time.

While the song brought the band notoriety, it also brought them into court. It seems the blues rhythm ZZ Top used in the song was the same rhythm used in John Lee Hooker's *Boogie Chillen* and the person who held the rights to *Boogie Chillen* filed a copyright infringement lawsuit against ZZ Top. The court ultimately ruled that the rhythm was part of the public domain.

LaGrange is played at nearly every ZZ Top concert and is combined with another song called *LaGrange/Sloppy Drunk Jam* that stretches for about 10 minutes.

LaGrange is a real place - LaGrange, Texas - and the shack described in the song is also a real place. That "shack outside LaGrange" is a brothel later referred to as the Chicken Ranch.

The brothel was not only the subject of a Broadway play but also the movie Best Little Whorehouse In Texas starring Burt Reynolds and Dolly Parton.

Livin' On A Prayer

There has always been wide speculation about the meaning behind Bon Jovi's *Livin' On A Prayer*.

Livin' On A Prayer appears on the band's 12-time platinum album Slippery When Wet. As a single the song sold 800,000 copies.

The song is about a fictional working-class couple, Tommy and Gina who are struggling to make ends meet while trying to maintain their relationship. As the lyrics say, "Tommy used to work on the docks, because the union's been on strike he's down on his luck." The song also makes reference to Gina working at a diner.

There is one faction that believes the song is pro-labor with the union striking for better pay and conditions. Others believe the song is anti-labor which tells of bosses forcing the union to go on strike.

John Bon Jovi said he wrote the song during the Reagan era and that President Reagan's trickle-down economics was at least in part behind the writing of the song.

Livin' On A Prayer was played at the concert for New York City in the aftermath of the 9-11 attack.

The song was also adopted by the George Mason University pep band when the school made its improbable run to the Final Four of the 2006 NCAA Men's Division One basketball tournament. The song became George Mason's unofficial theme song to represent the success of the underdog.

Take A Walk With Lou Reed

The characters Lou Reed sings about in his *Take A Walk On The Wild Side* are real people.

Holly was Holly Woodlawn, a transgender actress as was Candy Darling. Joe was a sex symbol in the gay culture. All three were superstars in Andy Warhol movies. Jackie was Jackie Curtis who performed in drag.

The character referred to as Little Joe is Joe Campbell who has connections to two infamous events in American history. He was said to be the lover of San Francisco City Supervisor Harvey Milk. On November 27, 1978, Milk and San Francisco Mayor George Moscone were murdered by another board supervisor named Dan White.

Another of Little Joe's alleged lovers was an ex-Marine named Oliver Billy Sipple. On September 22, 1975 Sipple went to San Francisco's Union Square to hear President Gerald Ford speak. Sipple just happened to be standing next to Sara Jane Moore who pulled out a revolver and aimed it at the president. Sipple knocked the gun away and the bullet went wild lodging into a building. Sipple's act may have saved President Ford's life.

Lunatic Fringe

Canadian band Red Rider's *Lunatic Fringe* has its roots in hatred and murder.

Guitarist Tom Cochrane said he wrote the song after becoming concerned about the resurgence of anti-Semitism in the 1970's. He said he was inspired by a book about Raoul Wallenberg who rescued Jews from the holocaust.

With that in mind, the lyrics: "Lunatic fringe, I know you're out there. You're in hiding and you hold your meetings. We can hear you coming. We know what you're after. We're wise to you this time. We won't let you kill the laughter."

There had been speculation that Cochrane's inspiration for the song was John Lennon's murder. Cochrane dispelled that theory saying he had written the song before Lennon was killed. However, Lennon's death played a role in the release of the song. Cochrane was told by the recording company that *Lunatic Fringe* did not have enough commercial appeal and could not be released as a single. Despite this, Cochrane was determined to release the song as a single because the day he recorded the demo for *Lunatic Fringe* was the day Lennon was murdered.

Yasgur's Farm

We all know very well what happened at Yasgur's Farm. What few of us know is the story behind the owner of the farm, Max Yasgur.

Max B. Yasgur studied real estate law at New York University before making a career turn and taking over the family's dairy farm. By the late 60's he was the largest milk producer in Sullivan County, New York with 650 cows.

When the producers of the Woodstock Music and Arts Fair were turned down by two neighboring towns, Max rented one of his fields to them for $50,000. Max needed the money because it had been a wet year and the crops were curtailed. Max's son Sam who was an assistant district attorney in Manhattan said his father also believed strongly in the freedom of expression and was angered by the hostilities of some townspeople toward "anti-war hippies." In fact, some in the community of Bethel erected signs that said "Stop Max's Hippie Music Festival" and "No 150,000 hippies here. Buy no milk."

When some of those neighbors tried to sell water to people coming to the concert, Max put up a big sign on his barn that read, "Free water" and according to son Sam, slammed his work-hardened fist on the table and demanded of some friends, "How can anyone ask money for water?" Max then told his farmhands to "take every milk bottle from the plant, fill them with water and give them to the kids and give away all the milk and milk products we had at the dairy."

Max Yasgur's famous "I'm a farmer" speech came on day three of the festival just before Joe Cocker's performance.

Max sold the farm in 1971 and moved to Florida where he died a year-and-a-half later of a heart attack. He was 53. He was given a full-page obituary in Rolling Stone Magazine, one of the few non-musicians to receive such an honor.

Max will forever be remembered through the lyrics of Crosby, Stills, Nash and Young's *Woodstock*: "Well I came upon a child of God, he was walking along the road and I asked him, tell me where are you going? This he told me, I'm going down to Yasgur's Farm...."

Ozzy's Comin' Home

Ozzy Osbourne's *Momma I'm Comin' Home* is his only solo single to make it to Billboard Magazine's Hot 100 chart, peaking at number 28. His only other Top 40 single was a duet he did with Lita Ford - *Close My Eyes Forever*.

The lyrics to *Momma I'm Comin' Home* give the impression that he was singing a ballad to his mother. However, considering who wrote the song, one comes to the realization it was not about Ozzy's mother at all! The song was co-written with his lead guitarist and Black Label Society heavy metal frontman Zak Wylde.

Momma is the nickname Ozzy gave to his wife and manager Sharon Osbourne. The power ballad is about his return to her following his imminent retirement.

Keith Moon

It was once said that what Jimi Hendrix was to guitar, The Who's Keith Moon was to drums.

Moon had a wild side as evidenced by an incident at his birthday party in 1968 when he drove his Lincoln limousine into the swimming pool. Moon made a run for it when police arrived but was caught when he slipped on a piece of his own birthday cake. Lead singer Roger Daltry attested to the incident saying, "We got the $50,000 bill for it."

Moon also had a bad habit of flushing cherry bombs down hotel toilets which got him banned for life from Holiday Inn, Sheraton and Hilton hotels.

The craziness came to an end in London on September 7, 1978. Moon woke at 7:30 that morning, watched some television, ate a steak and went back to bed. Later, his girlfriend tried to wake him and could not. Keith Moon was dead at age 32 from an overdose of a drug prescribed to him to combat alcoholism. There were 32 tablets in his system, 26 of which were undissolved.

Perhaps strangest of all is where Moon died. He was in a London flat that belonged to Harry Nilsson of *Everybody's Talkin' At Me* and *Without You* fame. It was the very same flat where four years earlier in 1974 Mamma Cass Elliot died.

Nazareth

When the band started in Dunferline, Scotland in 1961 they went by the name The Shadettes. In 1968 they changed their name to Nazareth and by 1972 they were on tour with Deep Purple.

In April of 1975 they recorded their album Hair of The Dog. Ironically, rock fans would always know the title song of the album by a different name, "Now you're messin' with a son of a bitch."

One of Nazareth's other hits was actually done first by two unlikely acts. The song was *Love Hurts* and was Nazareth's only Top-10 U.S. hit. The song was originally recorded by the Everly Brothers and later covered by Roy Orbison.

Things began to fall apart for the band as a result of lead singer Dan McCafferty's health. At age 66 he collapsed on stage in Canada due to a burst stomach ulcer. Three months later he got just three songs into a show in Sweden and had to leave again. It was at that point he quit. In his words, "I can't keep on doing this to the band."

The name Nazareth came from Nazareth, Pennsylvania. The band's classic song *The Weight* begins with the lyrics, "I pulled into Nazareth..."

Night Ranger

Night Ranger started out in the early 1980's under the name Ranger. In 1982 they changed their name to Night Ranger after a country band named The Rangers claimed trademark infringement.

Night Ranger's hit songs include *You Can Still Rock In America, When You Close Your Eyes* and *Don't Tell Me You Love Me.* The band also had a lesser-known hit with *Goodbye* written by guitarist Jack Blades in memory of his older brother who died of a heroin overdose. When Blades left the band he would go on to form Damn Yankees with Ted Nugent and Tommy Shaw of Styx.

Another of Night Ranger's hits was *Sister Christian* which peaked at number five in June of 1984. The song was written for band member Kelly Keagy's younger sister Christine and while the song was written in 1982 it was not released until 1984 because the band was concerned about losing their hard rock credentials.

Sister Christian is a cautionary anthem for girls across conservative middle America warning them not to 'give it up' before their time is due. As the song's second verse urges, "keep motorin'" instead.

John Michael Osbourne

John Michael Osbourne was born December 3, 1948 in Aston, Birmingham, England. The fourth of six children, his father was a nightshift toolmaker and his mother was a factory worker. Since grade school his nickname was Ozzy but it should be noted that his first wife, Thelma would only call him John.

Young Ozzy grew up with dyslexia, attention deficit disorder as well as other learning disabilities. At 15 he left school and held such jobs as construction worker, trainee plumber, apprentice toolmaker, car factory horn-tuner and even slaughterhouse worker. He once turned to crime. He stole a television and some clothing and ended up serving six months in Winson Green Prison.

When his music career finally took off and he was in search of a new manager he came across a man named Don Arden whose daughter was the company receptionist. Ozzy was immediately attracted to her but he felt she thought he was a lunatic. Don's daughter's name was Sharon - the future Mrs. Osbourne.

One of Ozzy's career lowlights happened when he met with the head of CBS Europe in Germany. Ozzy was drunk and thought he'd lighten up the mood by doing a striptease on the table. Later, since he was too drunk to remember, Sharon informed him that what he had actually done was a Nazi goosestep atop the table before dipping his family jewels in and then urinating in the executive's glass of wine.

Ozzy's first experience with cocaine was in 1971 at a hotel in Denver after a Black Sabbath show he had done with Mountain. Mountain guitarist Leslie West is said to have introduced him to the drug but West is reluctant to take credit. However, more than 40 years later the two remained close enough to have recorded a remake of Mountain's *Mississippi Queen* together.

Tom Petty

Born in Gainesville, Florida, Tom Petty's interest in rock music began at the age of 10 when he met Elvis Presley! Petty's uncle was working on the set of a Presley movie and invited Tom to watch the shoot. Soon after that meeting, Tom traded his Whamo slingshot for a friend's collection of Elvis Presley 45's. One of Petty's first guitar teachers was Don Felder who would later join the Eagles.

Beside being the frontman for Tom Petty and The Heartbreakers, he was also a member of the Travelling Wilburys. He was inducted into the Rock and Roll Hall of Fame in 2002.

Petty had a difficult relationship with his father who found it hard to accept that his son was interested in the arts. His father subjected Tom to verbal and physical abuse on a regular basis.

Petty has been married twice. The first time for 23 years, the second in 2001. He has two daughters and one stepson.

On May 17, 1987 an arsonist set fire to Petty's house in Encino, California. Firefighters were able to salvage the basement recording studio and some original tapes. However, his signature gray top hat was destroyed. Petty later rebuilt the house with fireproof materials.

Pink Floyd

The iconic Pink Floyd were originally known as the Tea Set until band member Syd Barrett came across an album that featured the names of two blues musicians, Pink Anderson and Floyd Council.

Rock and roll music makes for strange bedfellows as evidenced by the fact that when Pink Floyd played their first concert in 1971 they were joined on the bill by Buffy Sainte Marie and The 1910 Fruitgum Company of *Simon Says* and *1,2,3 Red Light* fame.

It is estimated that one in every twelve people in the world has a copy of the Pink Floyd album, Dark Side Of The Moon.

Rock fans have always been intrigued and curious about the ending of the song *Young Lust* which features a telephone operator. The song, which is on the album The Wall tells the story of Pink, a rock star away from home in search of wealth and fame and who has casual sex with groupies. He places a telephone call to his wife who is at their home in England and a man answers at which time Pink realizes his wife is cheating on him.

The album's co-producer, James Gutherie, wanted realism in the phone call so he placed a call from Los Angeles to his neighbor in London. The operator was real but she did not know she was being recorded. A little-known fact is that the operator that is heard on the song is actually the second operator they tried. It seems they had deemed the first operator's reaction as unsatisfactory.

Purple Haze

There are several theories as to the origin of Jimi Hendrix' *Purple Haze*. Herein is another for your consideration.

Purple Haze first appeared on the Jimi Hendrix Experience debut album in March of 1967. Most people assumed it was just another Jimi Hendrix drug song since Purple Haze was the street name for a certain type of drug and was also the name given to a cloud of pot smoke at a concert.

But another theory asserts the origin of the song had its roots in London when Hendrix read a bizarre newspaper story about a waitress who became obsessed with a regular cafe customer and she began stalking the man after he left the café where she worked.

The story goes that the woman slipped LSD into the man's cup of coffee and with his faculties diminished, the waitress led the man back to her apartment where she tied him up and held him captive for several days.

Hendrix was struck by the story and wrote the song from the perspective of the man coming to his senses and wondering what was going on. Hendrix always refuted the simple interpretation that it was a drug song by pointing to the lyric, "Whatever it is, that girl put a spell on me. Help me. Help me."

Jet City Woman

When the band started in Seattle in 1978 they went under the name The Joker, then Crossfire and after that The Mob after the Black Sabbath song *The Mob Rules.*

In 1982 their manager encouraged them to change their name so they named themselves after the first song on their demo tape, *Queen of The Reich* and Queensryche was born.

The band spent almost as much time in court as they did on stage. It seems the band split up and both warring factions took the name Queensryche until a judge eventually settled the matter. Things got so nasty and divisive that the band even fired vocalist Jeff Tate's daughter from running the band's fan club.

In 2010 the band almost broke up for good, but not by their own doing. They were performing for U.S. troops in Iraq when the base where they were playing came under attack. Bombs fell everywhere but fortunately no one was hurt.

Queensryche has had 13 studio albums with sales of 20 million.

One of their most popular songs is *Jet City Woman.* The song is about a woman coming home after a long trip. Jet City is the nickname for Seattle, the band's hometown. The song was written about band member Jeff Tate's first wife who was a flight attendant.

Quiet Riot

Founded in 1973 by guitarist Randy Rhodes, Quiet Riot is best known for their hit songs *Cum On Feel the Noyz* and *Metal Health*. It was Rhodes who auditioned for Black Sabbath in 1979 and Ozzy Osbourne hired him on the spot.

Rhodes and lead singer Kevin DuBrow gave the band its unique sound and by the mid-70's they were opening for Van Halen. Quiet Riot is ranked number 100 on VH1's 100 Greatest Artists of Hard Rock. Rhodes died in a plane crash in 1982.

DuBrow died of a cocaine overdose in his Las Vegas apartment in December, 2007. He had been dead for 6 days before anyone found him.

When Quiet Riot was founded they went by the name Mach 1. It was in May, 1975 that the band was having a conversation with Rick Parfitt who was a member of Status Quo who had a hit with *Pictures of Matchstick Men*. During that conversation, Parfitt said he'd like to name a band Quite Right. However, with his thick British accent it sounded like he was saying Quiet Riot - and the name was born.

Personal note: Our wedding in January of 1984 was in Milwaukee and we spent the night at the Sheraton Hotel in downtown Milwaukee. We checked into the hotel and went to the elevators. Suddenly there was screaming, crowds and pushing near our elevator. It seems Quiet Riot had just played a concert in downtown Milwaukee and they were staying at the same hotel. My new wife and I along with our two-year-old son found ourselves on the elevator with Quiet Riot. Our two-year old's favorite song was *Cum Feel The Noise* and his favorite band member was the drummer, the guy with the curly long hair – the guy my son called The Poodle. I was holding my son and we were standing next to The Poodle when my son reached out to touch The Poodle's hair. The Poodle said "hi" which scared my two-year old. I told the band we were big fans to which Kevin DuBrow said, "We didn't think people as old as you liked our stuff." (I was 32 years old!).

After we all checked into our rooms, my new family and Quiet Riot met at the hotel bar. My son sat on the bar, and banging my Budweiser beer bottle on the bar began singing *Cum Feel The Noise* much to the amazement of the band who joined in.

They Weren't The Ramones

The band formed in 1974 in Forest Hills, New York. It was comprised of John Cummings and Thomas Erdelyl who were with a group called Tangerine Puppets. Cummings and Erdelyl joined forces with Douglas Colvin and Jeffrey Hyman from Sniper. It is understandable if those four names are not familiar to you. Each band member would eventually change his name - first name and last.

The four would perform 2,263 concerts over the 22 years they were together. Eight years after they broke up in 1996 three of the four - Joey, Johnny and Dee Dee would be dead.

The Ramones were never brothers in real life. Douglas Colvin was the first to adopt the name 'Ramone', calling himself Dee Dee Ramone.

Colvin was inspired by Paul McCartney's use of the pseudonym Paul Ramone during his Silver Beatle days.

A Short Trip On The Speedwagon

REO Speedwagon was formed in 1967.

The band was named after a truck that one of the band members was studying in a transportation history class at the University of Illinois in Champagne.

The name of the truck was the Speedwagon.

R.E.O. are the initials of the Speedwagon's inventor, Ransom E. Olds.

Mick Ronson

Born in Yorkshire, England in 1946, Mick Ronson is best known as David Bowie's lead guitarist and was one of Ziggy Stardust's Spiders from Mars.

Ronson also did stints with Mott the Hoople and Van Morrison and later collaborated with Mott the Hoople founder Ian Hunter.

In Creem Magazine's 1974 poll of Best Rock Guitarists, Ronson placed second only to Jimmy Page. Eric Clapton placed third.

Ronson died of liver cancer in 1993 at the age of 46.

Without Mick Ronson there would be no *Jack And Diane* by John Mellencamp. Ronson was helping Mellencamp arrange some songs for an album. In Mellencamp's words, "I owe Mick Ronson the hit *Jack and Diane* as I had thrown it on the junk heap. Mick said, 'Johnny, you should put baby rattles on there.' I thought what the F does 'put baby rattles' on the record mean. So he put the percussion on there and he sang the part 'Let it rock, let it roll' as a choirish-type thing which had never occurred to me and that is the part that everybody remembers on the song. It was Ronson's idea."

7 Mary 3

This modern-day rock band got its name from a 70's cop show.

The band formed in 1992 when two college friends at the College of William and Mary in Williamsburg, Virginia got together, split the song-writing duties and formed an acoustic duo. Later they would take on a drummer and a bassist.

We know Seven Mary Three best for their hit *Cumbersome*. The name Seven Mary Three has its roots in television's 70's police series 'Chips' starring motorcycle officers Ponch and Johnny. Actor Erik Estrada was Ponch otherwise known as Officer Poncherella. His partner was Johnny - actor Larry Wilcox - Officer John Baker.

'7-Mary-3' was Officer John Baker's radio call sign - 7 designated the patrol beat, Mary designates that he is a motorcycle unit and three was his unit number.

Seven Mary Three band leader Jason Pollack said, "There's no great significance or anything. We were just tired of trying to think of a cool name."

Black Crows

The Black Crows song *She Talks To Angels* on their Shake Your Moneymaker album seems to be a song about a woman, pain and the drugs she uses to take the pain away. But where did the pain come from?

Black Crows lead singer Chris Robinson says the song is not about just one person but rather a compilation of people the band knew from the Atlanta club scene in their early days. Robinson said there was always a girl in the club scene with really dark makeup like Siouxsie and The Banshees. Thus the lyric, "She paints her eyes as black as night." Robinson then went on to write an entire song about this person including the dark details of drugs and escape.

Ironically, there was a Christian band that did a song about the Black Crows' *She Talks To Angels*. The Christian band's song was called *Black Bird* and tells of how the Black Crows need Jesus. One of the song's lyrics says, "You say you talk to angels, well I say it's such a lie."

In the Black Crows song, the woman seems to have an issue with Jesus as evidenced by the lyric, "She wears a cross around her neck. And the cross is someone she has not met. Not yet."

So what was her issue with Jesus? Where did the pain come from? Perhaps a clue is found in the lyric, "She keeps a lock of hair in her pocket - yes, the hair is from a little boy."

Is that little boy the angel she talks to? Was the angel a child she gave birth to and was either stillborn or short-lived?

Gimme Shelter

Rolling Stone Magazine said, "The Stones have never done anything better." They were referring to the song *Gimme Shelter* which appeared on the 1969 album Let It Bleed.

According to Mick Jagger, the song is about the very rough Vietnam War era with the violence, pillaging and burning. Said Mick, "It's kind of an end-of-the-world song."

The most interesting aspect of the song is who did and who did not sing backup vocals. The song's producer said the song needed a female backup so the call went out to Bonnie Bramlett. But Bonnie's husband Delaney would not let her sing with the Rolling Stones. Apparently Delaney, Bonnie and Friends were not friends with the Rolling Stones.

The Rolling Stones' producer then contacted backup singer Mary Clayton who had done backup work with Joe Cocker, Linda Ronstadt, Neil Young and she is also the female backup vocalist on Lynyrd Skynyrd's *Sweet Home Alabama*. Clayton also starred as the original Acid Queen in the first London production of The Who's Tommy.

Clayton was in bed when she got the call. Upon arriving at the recording session she belted out several takes. On the song's second refrain her voice cracks when she sings, "just a shot away" and it cracks again in the third refrain on the word "murder" after which Jagger is faintly heard exclaiming, "Woo!"

When the recording session ended, Clayton went back home, went back to bed and proceeded to have a miscarriage.

Wicked Lester

Chaim Witz was born in Haifa, Israel in 1949. When he was eight years old he and his mother emigrated to New York City while his father, Feri Witz remained in Israel where he had one other son and three daughters. In 2011, 54 years after he left, Chaim Witz went back to Israel where he would eventually meet his half-brother and three half-sisters.

Before beginning his music career, Chaim held several jobs in the New York City area. He was an excellent typist and not only was he the assistant editor of the fashion magazine Vogue, but he was also a sixth grade teacher.

He formed several bands including Lynx, the Missing Links and Bullfrog Bheer. In the early 70's he met Stanley Harvey Eisen and the two formed a band called Wicked Lester. The two needed a drummer so they answered an ad placed by drummer Peter Criscoula. The three band members then placed an ad in The Village Voice seeking a guitarist. The ad was answered by Paul Frehley. Ace Frehley, Peter Criss, Paul Stanley and Gene Simmons. Kiss was born.

Simmons dated former Playboy playmate and actress Shannon Tweed for 28 years until they were married in 2011. Formerly he had live-in relationships with Cher and Diana Ross.

Simmons remains heavily involved in the politics of Israel. The bass guitarist known to most of us for his long tongue and his ability to breathe fire speaks not just English but also German, Hungarian and Hebrew.

The Night Skynyrd Died

It was a Wednesday night, October 20, 1977. Lynyrd Skynyrd had just played a show in Greenville, South Carolina and the band and their entourage were flying to Baton Rouge, Louisiana to perform for a crowd of 10,000 at Louisiana State University.

There were 26 people on board the plane when the pilot reported trouble over Gillsburg, Mississippi. Contact was lost and the plane crashed deep in the woods near a stream which made it difficult for rescuers to reach the site. Upon arrival they heard groans of pain. The plane had been split open. Some of the passengers were thrown from the plane, others were tossed to the front where rescuers heard shouts of "get me out!" Rescuers had to step on bodies to get to bodies.

Three and a half hours later, farmer Johnny Mote was putting some hay out when three bloody survivors who managed to get out came up to him and said, "We've got to get them out!"

When all was said and done, six of the 26 people on board were dead including Lynyrd Skynyrd lead singer Ronnie Van Zant, guitarist Steve Gaines and vocalist Cassie Gaines who was Steve's sister.

A spokesman at Southwest Medical Center where the victims were taken said identification of the victims was difficult. Not because the bodies were burned, disfigured or dismembered. Rather, at the time of the crash, some of the passengers were playing poker and had their wallets with all of their identification out on the table.

Smoke On The Water

That December 4, 1971 day found Deep Purple at a hotel in Montreux, Switzerland to record their Machine Head album. The hotel was situated on the waters of Lake Geneva.

The album recording was to have taken place following a Frank Zappa concert at the hotel casino. But during Zappa's show, someone fired a flare gun into the ceiling burning the casino down and destroying all of Zappa's equipment in the process. Thus, the lyric in *Smoke On The Water*, "Some stupid with a flare gun burned the place to the ground."

Deep Purple was then booked into another hotel - The Grand - which did not have the amenities of their last accommodations . Thus, the lyric, "We ended up at the Grand Hotel, it was empty, cold and bare."

They recorded the album at The Grand in the Rolling Stones' mobile studio which is why they included the lyric, "But with the Rolling truck Stones thing just outside, making our music there."

The lyric "Swiss time was running out" refers to the fact that the band was under a time deadline because their visas were running out.

The most intriguing part of the song is the identity of 'Funky Claude'. The lyric says, "Funky Claude was running in and out pulling kids out the ground." Funky Claude is Claude Nobs, co-founder of the prestigious Montreux Jazz Festival and the man who found The Grand hotel for Deep Purple. During the fire it was Claude and Frank Zappa who helped to get the kids out of the casino.

When the album was released Claude Nobs became known forever as Funky Claude.

Spoonman

Pearl Jam's *Spoonman* is the story of a real person whose name is Artis.

Pearl Jam and Soundgarden, two Seattle-based bands were working on the soundtrack for the 1992 film Singles. Pearl Jam bassist Jeff Ament had been put in charge of coming up with a name for a fictional band that would appear in the movie. Citizen Dick was eventually chosen for the name. Also on the list of potential names - Spoonman.

In real life, Spoonman is a street performer named Artis who played in the streets of Santa Cruz and later Seattle playing music with a set of spoons.

The song *Spoonman* features Artis playing the spoons on the song's bridge.

In fact, on the back cover of the album in the credits it says, Spoons: Artis The Spoonman.

Stairway To Heaven

Since 2008, Led Zeppelin's *Stairway To Heaven* has been played on the airwaves approximately 1,432,403 times although the last time Led Zeppelin played the song in concert was July 7, 1980 in Berlin.

Stairway To Heaven remains the biggest selling sheet music song in history. Most hits sell 10,000 to 15,000 copies of sheet music. *Stairway To Heaven* has sold more than one million.

The song was played at nearly every Led Zeppelin concert, omitted only on rare occasions when the shows were interrupted by technical problems or when there were curfew issues.

The song was born one evening as Robert Plant sat by the fire searching for spiritual perfection. The lyrics were influenced by a book Plant was reading called Magic Arts in Celtic by Lewis Spence. In the book there are references to May queens, pipers and bustling hedgerows.

Stay

The song *Stay*, covered by Jackson Browne actually has its roots in 50's doo-wop music.

Stay was a 1953 hit by Maurice Williams and the Zodiacs that is in the history books as the shortest single ever to reach the top of the American record charts. In fact, at just one minute and fifty seconds it was named as the Greatest Really Short Rock Song Of All Time by Digital Dream Door.

Jackson Browne's version of the song begs the audience to stay for an encore and includes an extensive playout.

Maurice Williams' original version had a much different meaning. Williams was 15 years old at the time and was trying to convince his date not to go home at 10 o'clock as she was supposed to. He lost the argument and as he would relate years later, "Like a flood the words just came to me."

You Can't Always Get What You Want

The Rolling Stones' *You Can't Always Get What You Want*, written by Mick Jagger and Keith Richards in November, 1968 was recorded at Olympic Studios in London and features the London Bach Choir at the open and close of the song.

The song appeared on the 1969 album Let It Bleed and was named as the 100th Greatest Song Of All Time by Rolling Stone Magazine in the magazine's list of the top 500 songs.

You Can't Always Get What You Want touches on love, politics and drugs. Love is embodied in the lyric, "She was practiced at the art of deception." Politics - "I went down to the demonstration to get my fair share of abuse." Drugs - "I went down to the Chelsea drug store to get your prescription filled."

When most people hear the drugstore lyric, "I was standing in line with Mr. Jimmy and man did he look pretty ill" they think it is a reference to Jimi Hendrix. Rolling Stone Magazine writer David Dalton says Mr. Jimmy actually refers to Jimmy Miller, the producer of several Rolling Stones albums.

Jimmy Miller plays another important role in the song. Rolling Stones drummer Charlie Watts couldn't get the hang of the beat of the song so the song features producer Jimmy Miller on drums.

Sundown

Born in Ontario, Canada in 1948 Cathy Evelyn Smith served time in the California State Prison system for manslaughter. Her crime? She was the person who supplied the drugs to comedian John Belushi that killed him.

Rock music fans know Cathy Evelyn Smith by another name as well. It was in the 70's when she joined up with a famous musician. She was a back-up singer for him, co-wrote songs with him and even drove the tour bus. She was also said to be this married singer's mistress which led to the singer's divorce - said to be the most expensive in Canadian history.

The musician-mistress relationship weighed heavily on the musician which led him into the world of drugs. He knew he had to end the relationship and when he did he wrote a song about her. The beginning lyrics to the song are, "I can see her lyin' back in her satin dress in a room where you do what you don't confess. Sundown, you'd better take care if I find you been creepin' 'round my backstairs."

The musician was Gordon Lightfoot. Cathy Evelyn Smith is Sundown.

Mommy's Alright! Daddy's Alright!

Cheap Trick's *Surrender* is a teen anthem about a kid who thinks of his parents as a bit overprotective and kind of weird until that one night: "When I woke up Mom and Dad were rollin' on the couch. Rollin' numbers, rock and rollin', got my Kiss records out."

The band first played *Surrender* when they were rehearsing in the basement of guitarist Rick Nielsen's father's music shop on 7th Avenue in Rockford, Illinois. But when the song was released, one of the lyrics had to be changed. This was 1978 and there were certain lyrics that radio stations of the time were just not going to play. The lyric in question is where the young man tells about his mother serving in the Women's Air Corps or the WACS. The made-for-radio lyric says, "Now I had heard the WACS recruited old maids for the war."

The original lyric said, "Now I had heard the WACS were either old maids, dykes or whores."

The Who

One of the highlights of Woodstock was the performance by The Who. However, something happened during that performance that didn't make it to the movie or the album. There is a reference to it earlier in this book in the chapter titled Woodstock Lineup. The listing of The Who's set includes something called 'Abbie Hoffman incident'.

As The Who was performing at Woodstock on that Sunday morning, Yippie leader Abbie Hoffman was sitting on stage with concert organizer Michael Lang. Hoffman had been working in the medical tent since the opening of the festival. He was also high on LSD.

Hoffman had become increasingly determined to call attention to the plight of a man named John Sinclair who had been given a 10-year prison sentence for passing two marijuana cigarettes to an undercover narcotics officer.

Hoffman jumped on stage during a brief break in The Who's performance, grabbed the microphone and shouted, "I think this is a pile of shit while John Sinclair rots in prison!" Who lead guitarist Pete Townsend yelled at Hoffman, "Fuck off. Fuck off my fucking stage" and struck Hoffman with his guitar. Hoffman jumped off stage and disappeared into the crowd.

Thin Lizzy

Thin Lizzy was formed in 1969 when Eric Bell and Eric Wrixon went to a bar to see a band called Orphanage featuring vocalist Phil Lynott and drummer Brian Downey. While Bell and Wrixon's names are not familiar to us, they came from good stock. At the time, they were with a group called Them fronted by Van Morrison.

The four decided to form a group and took their name from a comic book character Tin Lizzy. They inserted the 'h' to play on the Irish accent's propensity to drop the 'h'.

As with many bands, success led to problems and on January 4, 1986 Phil Lynott died of drug dependency issues at age 36.

Twenty-seven years later, Lynott played a part in American political history. Lynott's mother and widow objected to Republican presidential candidate Mitt Romney's use of *The Boys Are Back In Town* during Romney's election campaign.

Said Lynott's mother Philomena, "As far as I'm concerned, Mitt Romney's opposition to gay marriage and to civil unions for gays makes him anti-gay which is not something Phillip would have supported."

Bad To The Bone

Music was not George Thorogood's first love. Born in 1950 in Delaware, Thorogood played second base on a late-70's baseball team in the Roberto Clemente League and was even named Rookie of the Year.

However, after seeing a performance by blues artist John P. Hammond, baseball took a backseat to music.

Most rock fans know Thorogood for his song *Bad To The Bone* which was used in a 1984 Buick advertising campaign. But George Thorgood and his band will go down in history for doing something that had never been done before and probably never will again. They did what they called the 50-50 Show.

It began with a show in Colorado, then a plane to Hawaii, the next night in Alaska and on to Washington State. Fifty shows in 50 states in 50 days.

Tom Sawyer

Rush's *Tom Sawyer* was released in 1981 and was named the 19th Greatest Hard Rock Song Of All Time by VH1 in 2009.

The song's original name was not *Tom Sawyer* but rather *Louis The Lawyer*. It was at a farm outside Toronto where the three members of Rush were on break from rehearsals when a friend of theirs gave them a poem called Louis The Lawyer. Rush played with it, changed it and turned the poem into the story of a modern-day rebel, a free spirit individualist striding the world wide-eyed and purposeful.

Although the song has an esteemed place in rock history, the band claims they did not put too much work into it. In a 2007 interview, guitarist Alex Lifeson, describing his guitar solo on *Tom Sawyer* said, "I winged it. Honest. I came in, did five takes, then went off and had a cigarette. I'm at my best for the first two takes."

She's A Beauty

At first listen, the Tubes' *She's A Beauty* sounds like a hard rock love song as exemplified by the lyric, "She's a beauty. She's one in a million girls." But in reality, the song is about an encounter with a stripper. Thus, the lyric, "But don't fall in love."

The MTV video of the song showed a young boy in a carnival car riding past a mermaid, a female trapeze artist and prehistoric women dressed in furs with the song's theme being he is attracted to them but he can never reach them. At the end of the ride when he gets off he is an old man with the message being this is the emotional and financial cost of falling in love with a stripper or prostitute or other type of sex worker.

Tubes frontman Fee Waybill said the song got its start when he was walking down a street in San Francisco and passed a booth outside a message parlor that had a sign on it that said, "Pay a dollar, talk to a naked girl." Waybill tells of the frustrating conversation that ensued between him and the woman inside the booth which led to the lyric, "She'll give you every penny's worth, but it will cost you a dollar first."

Wishing Well

Warrant's *Uncle Tom's Cabin* is the tale of two men witnessing a crime they wished they had never seen.

Uncle Tom had a cabin in the swamps of Louisiana where he would take his nephew fishing. The sheriff in town was crooked and he and a deputy killed two people and brought the bodies to the deepest part of the swamp known as the Wishing Well. They threw the bodies into the water and let them sink down so they would never be found.

Uncle Tom and his nephew were fishing that night and they saw the whole thing. Their dilemma was to-tell or not-to-tell.

The answer comes in one of the last lines of the song when Uncle Tom says, "Keep your mouth shut, that's what we're gonna do. Unless you want to wind up in the Wishing Well too."

Van Halen

Jan Van Halen was an accomplished saxophonist and clarinetist. His two sons, Eddie and Alex were quite the accomplished musicians themselves. On Van Halen's album Diver Down the brothers invited their father to play clarinet on their cover of *Big Bad Bill*. Jan Van Halen, a longtime alcoholic died at age 66.

Jan made sure the brothers took music lessons and both started out playing classical piano. Later, Alex would switch to flamenco guitar and Eddie acquired a drum kit.

While Eddie was out delivering newspapers, Alex would sneak sessions on Eddie's drums until Eddie one day found out and in frustration told Alex, "OK, you play drums and I'll go play your guitar!"

How Van Halen ever made it at all is a story in itself. In 1976, popular Los Angeles disc jockey Rodney Bingenheimer took Gene Simmons of Kiss to see Van Halen. Simmons then produced a Van Halen demo tape and he wanted the band to change its name to Daddy Longlegs. However the band decided to stick with the name Van Halen.

Simmons' involvement with Van Halen ended when he took their demo tape to Kiss' manager Bill Aucoin who told Simmons, "They had no chance of making it."

Stevie Ray Vaughn

Stevie Ray Vaughn was killed in a helicopter crash at Alpine Valley in East Troy, Wisconsin on August 27, 1990. He had just played two shows with Eric Clapton and the helicopter slammed into a hillside shortly after takeoff. Herein are excerpts from the Walworth County coroner's report.

The feet are covered by cowboy boots which are two-toned black and white.

A gold ring of an Indian mounted on a horse with the date 1904 is noted on the finger.

The right pants pocket contains a key which is apparently a motel key numbered 4007.

A smaller key which is labeled bar key number 942x is attached.

In the left pocket, three dimes, three pennies and two triangular-shaped picks with the name Stevie Ray Vaughn.

In the right rear pocket a wallet which contained a drivers license issued by the Texas Department of Public Safety upon which is a picture of the deceased.

There is also a Blockbuster membership card issued to Stevie Ray Vaughn. There is an American Express Card, a Citibank Card and a frequent flyer miles card. The wallet contains one $20 bill, two $5 dollar bills and a $1 dollar bill.

Also in the right rear pocket, a black, unbreakable comb.

On the shoulder of the leather jacket is a patch that says 'Eric Clapton Band'.

In the left front pocket a wad of bills. A 10, 20, 50 and 6 100-dollar bills all wet and stained with kerosene.

The left ring finger has a gold ring which is apparently made from a coin. The left wrist also has a Juan Jean watch and a rather heavy gold-plated band.

The head is symmetrical and is covered with long, dark hair.

Bang A Gong

Marc Bolan was the frontman and lead guitarist for the glam rock band T-Rex, best known for their iconic hit *Get It On, Bang A Gong*. This is a tale of the night Bolan met his untimely demise.

On the night of September 16, 1977, Bolan and girlfriend Gloria Jones were heading home in Bolan's Rolls Royce after a night at Morton's Drinking Club in southwest London.

They were less than two miles from home when the car went off the road and slammed into a sycamore tree killing Bolan instantly.

People like David Bowie and Rod Stewart came to his funeral.

Bolan's fascination with cars worked its way into many of his songs, like *Jeepster*. In *Get It On, Bang A Gong* there is a lyric that says, "We'll you're built like a car, you've got a hub cap diamond star halo."

It is ironic that the then-29-year-old Bolan might be alive today had he been driving that night. But Gloria was driving and she only broke her arm and jaw.

It should be noted that Bolan could not have driven the car that night. No, he was not drunk. Marc Bolan did not have a drivers license. He never learned how to drive because he feared premature death.

Fred Bear

The song makes Fred Bear appear to be a fictional character, but Fred Bear was very real. He was born March 5, 1902 in Waynesboro, Pennsylvania and died April 27, 1988 in Gainesville, Florida.

He didn't start doing what he was best known for until he was 29 years old. It was then he got good at it. Bowhunting.

He went on to become a world traveler, film producer, founder of an outdoor sports company and there would eventually be a museum in Grayling, Michigan that bears his name.

He was Ted Nugent's friend. They bowhunted together. In song, Nugent calls upon his friend's spirit when he says, "We're not alone in the great outdoors. We got his spirit, we got his soul. He will guide our steps and our arrows home. I'm glad to have you at my side my friend and I'll join you in the big hunt before too long."

Ted was singing about his friend Fred. Not a fictitious character, but someone who actually existed. Fred Bear.

Johnny Allen

His mother Lucille was just 17 when Johnny Allen was born in 1942. She always called him Buster. When Buster's two baby brothers were born Dad walked out on Lucille and the children. Lucille died in 1958 and Buster then lived with relatives and acquaintances.

Buster taught himself to play guitar, first by strumming his father's broom.

Buster would later turn to crime and was given a choice by a judge - jail or two years in the Army. Buster chose the Army but was discharged a year later because of discipline problems.

Buster became proficient enough at playing guitar that he played backup for Little Richard, Sam Cooke and the Isley Brothers.

He bought some of his outlandish stage clothes from designer Chris Jagger - Mick Jagger's brother.

Buster had fun with fans who seemed to mishear one of his lyrics. Onstage, Buster would point to bass player Noel Redding or drummer Mitch Mitchell when he sang, "S'cuse me while I kiss the sky (this guy)."

. Buster - Jimi Hendrix left us September 18, 1970.

Derringer

It was 1965 when a 17-year-old boy named Richard Zehringer formed a band called the McCoys. Their hit song *Hang On Sloopy* was so big in the summer of '65 that only the Beatles' *Yesterday* knocked it off the top of the charts.

The McCoys would go on to open for the Rolling Stones on their 1966 American tour.

Richard later played guitar in Johnny and Edgar Winter's bands, he is on Alice Cooper's Killer album, he opened for Led Zeppelin and performed many of the World Wrestling Federation songs including *Real American* which was Hulk Hogan's theme song.

He also appeared on a Kiss album, toured with Cyndi Lauper and in 2011 toured with Ringo Starr's All-Star Band.

Early in his career his band went through several name changes which included 'The Rick Z Combo' and 'Rick And the Raiders'. They settled on the name The McCoys when Bang Records signed them and released *Hang On Sloopy*.

Bang Records logo, by the way, was a derringer. Rick Derringer.

The Runaways

It was 1975 when four teenage girls formed a band called The Runaways and garnered substantial media attention thanks to their 'jailbait on the run' gimmick.

But The Runaways were more than a gimmick. They were good. Each band member had a special quality.

Cherie Curie was the lead vocalist whose downfall was drug addiction after the band broke up in 1979. In keeping with the tough-girl image, Curie would go on to become a woodcarving artist who used a chainsaw to create her works.

Drummer Sandy West has been described as the best female drummer of all time. She was a chain smoker who died of lung cancer in 2006 at the age of 47.

Rosanna Ford, one of the band's guitarists would change her first name to Lita. Lita Ford.

The other guitarist was Joan Marie Larkin, a girl who idolized Suzi Quatro so much that she would hang out at hotels just to watch Quatro walk by. She even imitated Quatro's shag haircut and platform shoes. Joan Marie Larkin would change her last name to Jett. Joan Jett.

Grace Slick

Born Grace Barnett Wing on October 30, 1939 in Evanston, Illinois she was of Norwegian and Swedish descent. Her ancestors can be traced back to the Mayflower. Her father was an investment banker and Grace went to a private all-girls school in California before she attended Finch College in New York and the University of Miami.

Grace also did some modeling, so when her husband formed the band The Great Society, Grace joined just for fun.

Later, another local band, Jefferson Airplane had lost their lead singer and asked Grace to join them. She brought with her two songs she said the wrote as a member of The Great Society, *Somebody To Love* and *White Rabbit* which she said she wrote in one hour.

The Jefferson Airplane version of *White Rabbit* is a bit different than The Great Society's version. With The Great Society, Grace was a musician and played oboe.

As a footnote, Grace Slick made television history during a 1969 appearance on The Dick Cavett Show as the first person to say "MF" on television.

Warren Zevon

Warren William Zevon was born January 24, 1947 to Beverly and William Zevon. William, Sr. was a bookie who handled bets for the notorious mobster Mickey Cohen.

The family moved to Los Angeles where young William was an occasional visitor to the home of none other than Igor Stravinsky, the Russian composer said to be the most important of our time.

As a session musician he wrote songs for The Turtles, wrote Linda Ronstadt's *Poor, Poor Pitiful Me* and toured with the Everly Brothers. After that tour he roomed with the then-unknown Lindsey Buckingham and Stevie Nicks.

His own compositions include *Werewolves of London* and *Lawyers, Guns and Money*.

He was a regular on The Late Show With David Letterman and sometimes even substituted for Letterman's bandleader Paul Schaffer. Zevon called Letterman the best friend his music ever had.

Zevon had a lifelong phobia of doctors and rarely received a medical assessment so it was perhaps no surprise that in 2000 he became ill and dizzy after a tour and was diagnosed with inoperable cancer of the abdominal lining.

On one particular Letterman show he told Dave, "I might have made a tactical error in not going to a physician for 20 years."

After that show Zevon gave Letterman the guitar he always used on the show and he made a single request of Dave, "Here, I want you to have this. Take good care of it."

Warren Zevon died September 7, 2003 in Los Angeles at the age of 56. He was cremated and his ashes were scattered over the Pacific Ocean.

On that last Letterman show, Dave asked Zevon if he knew something more about life and death now. Zevon's insightful answer, "Enjoy every sandwich."

"This is the end, beautiful friend."

The End, Doors

As with all books, something gets left out. Now that you have read about the songs and bands I've featured you are probably screaming, "He forgot ....." and "What about ......" and "Why didn't he include..." and "How could he have left out......?"

That's the great part about rock and roll music. Each of us has our own songs and bands that bring us back to that special place and time in our lives. Take heart! That special place and time is still there. It didn't go anywhere. You did!

What you may not realize is that in this world of quantum physics, a piece of you is still back there. It never left and your connection to that piece of you was never broken. It's always been there.

I implore you to find those childhood and teenage years songs. Play them. Get reacquainted with them. Feel the way they used to make you feel. It may have been 30, 40 and even 50 years since you were last at that time and place, but I promise you there is a *you* waiting there to see *you* again!

I have truly enjoyed our time together. I hope you did too.

Rock on.

Tom

Other Books By Tom Zalaski

The View From The Blanket – Weekapaug

If you own a cottage or have ever rented one at the ocean, the lake, a river or a resort get ready to relive the experience each time you open *The View From The Blanket*. Year 'round therapy to get you through your worst winter day at the office.

We Need To Do A Benefit Fundraiser – But How?

A loved one or friend is in need of financial help due to an illness, tragedy or unforeseen circumstance and you have taken it upon yourself to lead the way to get that person on their feet physically and financially. This is the step-by-step how-to book to coordinate that all-important benefit fundraiser.

How To Manipulate The Media For Fun And Profit

How to deal with the media in good times and bad. Media strategy for when your company has a strike, a stockholder revolt, a scandal, a product recall and even an accidental death. Also, how to get the media to cover your 'good stuff' like the check presentation, a groundbreaking, new product unveil and employee community involvement. Tips from Tom Zalaski from his 40 years of anchoring television newscasts!

Leave 'Em Speechless

Conquer your fear of public speaking now! Tom Zalaski has appeared before countless groups in his 40-year television career. Beside anchoring nightly television newscasts, Tom emcees events, conducts seminars and is a sought-after dinner speaker. This book doesn't require weeks of study or ask you to sign up for some expensive course. This is one-stop shopping.

You get it all, now! Tom will get you over your fear with an easy, practical and common sense approach.

Available at:
Amazon.com
Amazon kindle
Barnes and Noble
www.tomzalaski.com

www.ingramcontent.com/pod-product-compliance
Lightning Source LLC
Chambersburg PA
CBHW071002040426
42443CB00007B/629